MURRY BURNHAM'S HUNTING SECRETS

MURRY BURNHAM'S HUNTING SECRETS

by Murry Burnham
with Russell Tinsley

WINCHESTER PRESS
An Imprint of New Century Publishers, Inc.

Printing Code
11 12 13 14 15 16

Library of Congress Cataloging in Publication Data

Burnham, Murry.
  Murry Burnham's Hunting secrets.

  1. Hunting. I. Tinsley, Russell.   II. Title.
SK33.B897   1983   799.2   83-13315
ISBN 0-8329-0343-4

Dedication

To my late father J. Morton Burnham, for his patience and wisdom while teaching a curious kid what hunting is all about, and to my mother Pauline Burnham, who tolerated this hunting nonsense when she thought I should be taking care of my chores. Without both, this book would not have been possible. And a special salute to my wife Jolene for her love and understanding.

Contents

Acknowledgments

My appreciation to the many outdoor writers, who didn't make me a better hunter but certainly made me better known; to the ranchers who have trusted me on their lands; and to friends who have been a source of encouragement. To list them all would be an injustice since I surely would overlook someone deserving. You know who you are and I say thanks.

MURRY BURNHAM'S HUNTING SECRETS

Introduction

Murry Burnham is a hunter-extraordinary. He is best known as a caller of wild animals and birds, but his expertise is much more diverse. It also includes a mastery of more basic skills, such as stand and still hunting, used on a wide variety of game both large and small. His hunting secrets come from years of study and personal experiences. He has spent much of his lifetime in the woods. Few details escape his inquisitive mind.

This is a primary reason he is a cut above the rest. He sees things that others overlook, pieces of a puzzle he puts together mentally. Despite his uncommon success and reputation, he admits he still is experimenting and learning. He is continually searching for the "why" of what creatures do and when they do it.

I have hunted with Murry for more than two decades. Spend that much time in a hunting camp and in the woods with a man and you learn a lot about him. Murry not only is a talented hunter, he is a concerned sportsman. I never have heard him even suggest violating the law. When he goes to another state to hunt he does his homework; he probably knows that state's game laws better than the local residents. As he stresses in later chapters, there are some states where night hunting is illegal, even when calling predators, and some states prohibit the use of electronic calling devices. Never go hunting without understanding what you can or cannot do. Respect the wildlife and the law.

When Murry comes home without game, it usually is by choice. I have seen him pass up bucks, both whitetails and mulies, that most of us would dearly love to have hanging on our walls. He probably has spent more time hunting with a camera than with rifle and bow.

To photograph wildlife, you must be observant, patient, and prepared. You must learn to anticipate what a wild critter will do. And to anticipate, you must know something about its behavioral patterns.

Murry Burnham knows.

We've camped and hunted together in such far-flung places as the remote backcountry of Mexico, in the Colorado mountains, along the rivers of Nebraska, and in the flat thornbrush sections of south Texas. Murry has provided me with some of my most memorable hunting thrills.

I recall the time, near the small town of Encinal in south Texas, when at daybreak Murry's rabbit-squeal call brought seven coyotes in from the brush. We could see them approaching in the distance from across a brush-cleared grassy plain. They came trotting, single file, as though they were being led on an invisible leash. They were no more than 15 yards away when they finally stopped to glance around.

One misty, cold night near Sweetwater, Texas, between nightfall and midnight Murry called five bobcats and I shot three of them. Murry also might remind me of another moonless night in south Texas when he called a lean and muscular cat within eight feet and I missed it. When he switched on the bright shooting light, the reflection from the stubby-tailed cat's pelt created a glare and all I could see was a splash of blinding brilliance through the scope. I pointed the rifle at the glare and fired. I could have done better with a baseball bat.

Once, not far from Laredo on the Texas-Mexico border, Murry rattled up the biggest whitetail buck I have ever seen. The heavy-antlered brute got away because I passed up a reasonable shot, looking for a better one. No excuses; I knew better. But that same morning, Murry rattled up the largest buck I have killed, not as big as the one that got away, but still a trophy.

There are other such stories, almost too numerous to remember. But one stands out, even though it happened almost 20 years ago. We were hunting near Murry's home in central Texas. It was nearing sundown when Murry directed me to sit against a tree. He hid himself in a brush clump a few yards away and went to work with a call.

I glanced around as the anguished man-made squeals filled the air, and almost immediately felt something heavy plop into my lap. There, inches away, was the face of a large raccoon. His forepaws were resting on my chest and we were eyeball-to-eyeball. I don't know which of us was more surprised or startled, but both of us moved pretty quick. I jumped up, and the 'coon did a back flip and hit the ground running. He disappeared into a ground burrow no more than 20 yards away.

The late Morton Burnham, Murry's father, had a more frightening experience. He was in a large live oak tree, sucking with his lips to imitate the cry of a crippled rabbit. Hunting only by the light of a full moon, he glimpsed movement below him and saw a lanky bobcat walk into the open.

In the excitement, Morton forgot that cats sometimes hunt in pairs. He was raising his shotgun to fire when a second bobcat, this one in the tree, ambushed him. Morton escaped with only a few scratches and a good case of the shakes as the cat immediately realized its mistake and scrambled out of the tree.

Morton Burnham was a remarkable man. Short and wiry, he could slink through the woods silent as smoke. In his younger years, deer were scarce in his part of Texas and a man had to hunt hard to score. When he found what he suspected was a fresh buck track, Morton would stay on the trail for days if need be, sleeping in the woods. More often than not he brought home venison.

Much of Murry's hunting knowledge came from his father. In a roundabout way, Morton was also responsible for Murry's commercial success. Murry was in his twenties and building fences for a few dollars a day, using all his money and spare time for hunting. He was happy but, he said, he wasn't facing much of a future.

A magazine article changed his life. *True* published a feature about his father's uncanny ability to call animals such as wolves and foxes by sucking with his lips to imitate rabbit distress cries. Hundreds of readers wrote to ask where they could buy such a call to attract predators. Neither Murry nor his brother Winston knew of a commercially available call, so they designed a simple device: two pieces of flat plastic with a rubber-band reed, the famous Burnham Bros. Short-Range Predator Call that's still on the market. Their initial endeavor was a "shade-tree" operation—literally. They would sit under a pecan tree in their backyard and assemble the calls by hand.

Eventually, Murry acquired Winston's share of the business. Burnham Bros. now ships thousands of these calls and related calling and hunting equipment worldwide each year.

—Russell Tinsley

Chapter 1

Become a "Lucky" Hunter

Let's shoot straight, right off. If you're just starting to hunt, don't expect me to offer any magic shortcuts to success. If you're already into hunting, but not satisfied with your results and hoping for a quick fix, you're going to be disappointed. I've spent most of my life hunting and I know you can benefit from my experience and know-how, but how successful you become will depend on how much you really want it. Hunting is not much different from most anything else; the result is in direct proportion to the effort. In short, you get there with dedication and hard work.

It's easy to dismiss successful hunters as lucky. Oh sure, I've had my share of good fortune. But if you work hard and spend a lot of time in the woods, these things are going to happen. The hunter who gets his game year after year isn't the beneficiary of divine grace; his luck is the result of preparation meeting opportunity.

Let me tell you how I make my luck. While working on this book, I took time out for a coyote-calling hunt in south Texas with my friend Bill McReynolds. We went to a large cattle ranch where I've hunted many times. I knew the country and I knew where to hunt. That's how "lucky" I am.

Learning your hunting country—the lay of the land—is important to success. A good area one year will most likely be a productive spot the next. You should spend more time following the trails and looking for signs than you do hunting or calling. Wild creatures

Luck does play a part in hunting. But if you're looking to put a trophy buck like this on your wall, effort and patience will account for more racks than "luck."

leave clues, and you must collect and analyze these clues to get a mental picture of what's going on. In later chapters I'll be more specific as to what to look for.

But back to my hunt with McReynolds. I knew where to stop the pickup and I knew the route to walk. Again, this is because I'd done my homework and was familiar with the country.

South Texas can fool you. This part, near Laredo on the Mexico border, is a mix of cacti and thornbrush. It doesn't look like much, but it's rich in wildlife. I can't think of another place that has more game, both in variety and numbers. It boasts everything from javelina, rabbits, and quail to whitetail deer, coyotes, and bobcats. The landscape is mostly flat with a few rolling "hills" that are really just high places—typically not more than 30 or 40 feet in elevation—but when you climb one you can see down into the thick cover. At ground level you can't see far in any direction.

Bill and I walked a brushy ditch, moving as quietly as possible. Coyotes have super hearing. If you go blundering through the woods you'll have luck all right—bad luck. Let a coyote know you're coming and your chances of calling him will be about as good as a streak of doubles on grouse.

After walking maybe a quarter mile, Bill and I angled out of the ditch and up the backside of a rolling hill. As we neared the top, we paused and slipped on camouflage headnets because human faces reflect light. If a coyote had been looking when we crested the hill, the flash would have spooked him.

We eased over the rise, bent low and moving slowly. We went down the slope a few feet before sitting, so our bodies wouldn't be silhouetted against the sky.

Bill got his .243 into position. When he decides to shoot, he doesn't waste motion. He knows that you've got to be prepared when opportunity comes—you know, "lucky."

I went to work with a call. I'd been calling for probably a little more than 10 minutes when Bill shot. Even though we'd been watching the same area, I hadn't seen the coyote—a big, old male—until Bill dropped him. Bill's shot didn't startle me because I knew something was coming. Just before his rifle boomed, two cottontails came scooting out of the underbrush. Something had frightened them, and that something turned out to be the coyote.

You must learn to interpret signs like this. Nature sometimes provides us with clues, but we have to recognize and take advantage of them.

I remember the first bear I shot. A friend and I were hunting the Uncompahgre National Forest of western Colorado. We got "lucky" by shouldering backpacks with bedding and food and hiking up the mountains maybe six or eight miles to the timberline, to get away from other hunters. We spread out our sleeping bags on heaps of pine needles. At that altitude the air is incredibly clear, and the stars seemed close enough to touch.

We were hidden on trails, watching, by first light. No wind was

My father, the late J. Morton Burnham, taught me much of what I know about calling and hunting. Dad worked out most of his problems himself and even invented his own headlamp, far more crude than this model, when he was a youngster.

blowing and the forest was quiet, but the October air was sharp and I was thankful for the warm jacket. You can't hunt when you're uncomfortable. You lose concentration and you need to be aware of what's going on at all times.

In this instance, the peaks behind me were silhouetted against a bright sky as daybreak slowly turned the gloom into individual shapes. I was careful to put the rising sun behind me to keep the glare from my eyes, but my first consideration was to check wind currents. In the high country, wind can be tricky, changing directions several times a day. If you don't have the breeze to your advantage, it's no use worrying about anything else. One whiff of human scent will spook any wild animal.

I was intently watching the trail when I heard the animal coming. The male black bear wasn't actually making noise, but a pine squirrel was really carrying on. The big-mouthed squirrel told me something was approaching and I was ready when the bear walked around a bend in the trail. I guess I got "lucky."

I can't overemphasize the need to be ready at all times. I don't know how often I've heard stories about how a hunter put his gun down to relieve himself or light a cigarette, and lost an opportunity for a shot. In hunting, you don't have the luxury of an instant replay. Chances are few, and you must take advantage of every one.

If you aren't comfortable, you'll be wiggling and squirming and unprepared. Before sitting down, I try to prepare for a long wait. If I'm going to be leaning against a tree and the earth is soft, I scrape a depression to fit my rear. This not only makes sitting more tolerable, but I don't continually slip away from the tree.

When trying to call a turkey in the spring, I often stand or sit in a bush, just high enough to conceal my body and where I can rest my shotgun across a limb. This way, if a gobbler shows, I can lean into the butt, aim, and squeeze the trigger, in one smooth motion. There's almost no movement for the sharp-eyed tom to detect.

My dad, J. Morton Burnham, was a master at this sort of thing. He preached the necessity of being as motionless as possible. Don't underestimate a wild animal's ability to detect anything unnatural. Even the slightest noise or movement can alarm an animal.

Dad's way of sitting looked uncomfortable, but he could remain in that position for hours. He'd tuck his left foot under him and lean against something solid with his right knee upturned. He could then rest his gun across his knee with the stock against his shoulder. Being a southpaw, he'd make rabbit distress cries with his lips and right hand while holding the gun with his left. If he wanted to cut down on reaction time, he'd release the gun safety. When a wild

Dad taught me the importance of being well hidden when hunting wary game. The tree crotch and backdrop provides a good cover, but camo gloves and pants would be even better in this situation.

animal showed up, all he had to do was aim and pull the trigger. The process involved virtually no movement.

Dad also taught me the value of concealment. When you get into position, find a place where you're comfortable and hidden, but still have a good field of view. Knowing something about the behavior of the species you're hunting will help in picking a stand. I've seen turkey hunters get back in heavy thickets to call. They're well concealed, but can't see. No wary gobbler will go into thick cover like that.

If a tree trunk is all that's available, I prefer to sit with my back against it. In green or dark scrubby bush, I push back into it and sit on some of the lower limbs. Some of the branches will be shielding my face and the rest of the bush will be behind me. I'll be hidden well enough to suit me and fool the game.

I'm convinced you can't be too careful. Any edge you get is to your advantage. But sometimes we overlook the obvious.

I recall a spring turkey hunt with Russell Tinsley, a longtime friend and hunting partner who helped put this book together. He was under a green bush and wearing camouflage clothing, complete with a headnet and camo gloves. But he overlooked his wristwatch, which had a shiny stretch-metal band. His shirt sleeve and glove top didn't quite meet, and there, shining in the light, was the band. I noticed it immediately, but Russell told me he was unaware the band was reflecting light. See what I mean about the little things?

But you aren't always sitting; occasionally you have to move about, and when you're moving you're going to make some noise. It's inevitable, so the only recourse is to minimize the impact.

A planned approach to the preselected spot—perhaps a deer stand or a place to call predators—is very important. Avoid being silhouetted atop a ridge. Pick a path you can walk with as little noise as possible. If you must talk, whisper. I prefer to communicate with hand signals. When there are two people, it also pays to stay in step, making it sound as though only one person is walking.

You'll be smart to move only if you must. When sitting motionless, you minimize human error. You eliminate noise, but, more importantly, you stop movement. The eyes of animals are conditioned to movement. Being motionless improves your odds.

Even when sitting, I don't forget why I'm there. I run imaginary

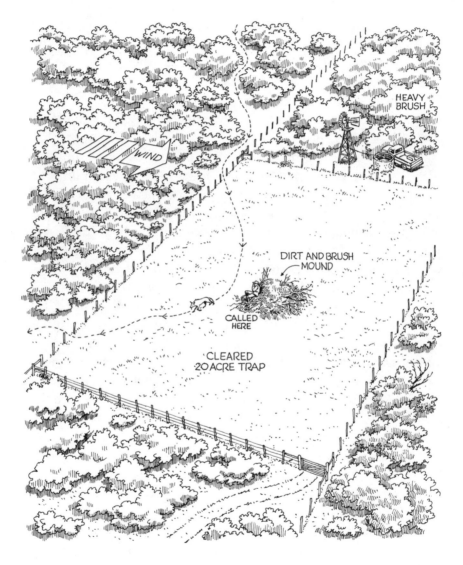

Look for a situation like this to bring a predator into the open. Note I parked my pickup out of sight at the windmill. The brush in the center of the field offered a place to hide with good visibility. I watch into the wind as I call.

14

But despite the wind, never completely ignore your backside. On this hunt in Texas near the Mexico border, a javelina came from downwind where I didn't see it, and it ran close and I thought for a moment it was going to attack.

15

If you plan on calling at night, do your scouting during the day and pick out your calling sites. Things look different at night, and you might stop at places where you have poor visibility.

situations through my mind, trying to anticipate most anything that might happen. I call this technique "programming" myself. When opportunity shows, your response has to be immediate. You can't make a foolish mistake. If you have to think about what to do, rather than reacting instinctively, you'll probably blow the chance for success.

Because I had such contingency plans worked out in my mind, I was able to shoot a huge six-point bull elk under conditions where most less-experienced hunters would have failed. I was hunting the Colorado high country, leaning against a tall ponderosa pine. It was late afternoon and a light breeze was rustling the treetops. Since I'd been sitting for most of the day, I'd had a lot of time to think and didn't let the hours go to waste. I knew what I'd do in most any situation.

I was watching out front when, from the corner of my eye, I caught movement behind me. Slowly I turned my head. Three or four elk were walking through the thick pine forest. Right away I saw one had a massive rack.

Since I'm left handed, I couldn't swing to the left to shoot. I'd already figured that out. Instead, I pivoted to my right, putting my right knee down and pulling my left leg up and over. The tree trunk between me and the elk kept me hidden. As I came around, my rifle was up and rested against the tree in the same continuous motion. I picked out a narrow opening in the direction the elk were traveling and put my scope sight on the big one. When the bull walked into view, I hit him solidly with a 7mm Magnum slug.

The bull whirled and stumbled down the opening. I didn't hesitate. I bolted in another round, aimed, fired, and finished the job.

Remember this: after you shoot, keep your gun up and ready. If the animal shows any life, don't hesitate to fire again. I've seen "dead" animals jump up and run off. Never assume anything—not if you want to get "lucky."

Chapter 2

Calling Sounds

I've always been fascinated by sounds that attract animals and birds. It all started with Dad.

In my opinion, he was the father of predator calling, the first to use rabbit distress cries to bring in wolves and foxes. It's logical, when you think about it. Some say the Indians started the practice, but until somebody proves differently, I'll say Dad gets the credit.

Dad was born with an inventor's flair. When he was only 10, he designed a light to strap to his forehead. He cut the front from a lard can and fastened two small snuff cans to the bottom. In each snuff can he put a little kerosene and a lamp wick. It didn't provide much light, but enough for Dad to see the trail he was following.

There was also enough faint illumination to see the reflection from an animal's eyes. It doesn't take much light to "pick up eyes," Dad later said.

He made the light for hunting deer. This was shortly after the turn of the century, and there were few game laws. Certainly there was no law prohibiting the jacklighting of deer since there were no effective means of doing this (flashlights and headlights came along later).

Back then, Dad's family hunted for food. In those innocent days, game was commonly taken by several methods that were later prohibited. For instance, in some regions hounds were used to drive

As shown in this photo, my father's methods worked. As far as I can determine, he was the one who developed the most successful techniques for calling predators.

deer into a lake or river, where they were killed from canoes. Dad never would have done anything unsporting—and no one would have considered his night light unsporting. On the contrary, his inventiveness was admired.

Later, as he matured and became more concerned, Dad became a hunter of big bucks, and in his last years he quit hunting and instead fed the deer. He'd walk into the big field in front of his house and rattle a bucket filled with corn. Deer—does and bucks—would come a-running from every direction. He had this thing with deer; they trusted him and would approach almost close enough for him to touch. Even big-antlered bucks would eat close by. But let a stranger go into the field with him and the animals immediately got skitterish.

Anyway, back to my story. As young Morton Burnham slipped furtively into the field, wearing his lamp, he spotted eyes in the soft glow of light. He also could make out the dim outline of a large deer. At point-blank range he blasted the buck with buckshot from his 12 gauge.

Then the unexpected happened. A jackrabbit squatting near the buck took off, fleeing to a nearby fence. When it tried to go under, the animal got entangled in the barbed wire and began screaming, the most pitiful cries Dad had ever heard.

Almost instantly three shadowy forms emerged from the darkness, running through the edge of Dad's light, ignoring him. The wolves went straight to the trapped rabbit and pounced on it, tearing and snarling.

Dad frantically tried to reload the single-shot shotgun, but the wolves were gone before he could chamber a shell.

Afterward, Dad began thinking about what he had seen. If wolves were attracted to a helpless rabbit, why couldn't he learn to imitate the distress cries and bring wolves within shooting range?

He started experimenting and practicing. About three months later he figured he had the sound down pat. He made the distress cries by squeaking with his lips, cupping his hand over his mouth to control the tone and pitch. Dad was eager to test his theory but he remembered, all too vividly, how those wolves had come rapidly out of the darkness, and he was a bit uneasy about it all. He talked another boy, slightly older, into going along.

They went through the same fence into the same field, but it was daylight this time. In the night, wolves can close in too quickly, too suddenly, but in the early morning light Dad wasn't afraid.

Dad was always a careful hunter, even in the beginning. He rarely took chances. Since the shotgun lacked range and firepower, this time he carried a .32-20 rifle, fully loaded. His companion also had a rifle to back him up.

They were standing, talking about what they should do, when across the field they saw a doe running for her life with seven wolves racing after her. In the plowed field the deer didn't have a chance. The animals soon overtook her and dragged her down. Six of the wolves did the killing while an old male walked a few steps toward the boys and stood guard.

Instead of trying to slip closer to the wolves, which were about

150 yards away, Dad grabbed the other boy's arm and pulled him behind a log lying at the edge of the field. Dad put his hand to his mouth and began calling. He was hoping the idea might work, but he sure didn't expect what happened next.

The old male came running at full speed. He had moved only a short distance when a she-wolf feasting on the deer looked up and, without hesitation, abandoned the carcass and gave chase. She quickly caught and passed the old male. Dad had the rifle resting over the log with the safety off. By this time the other wolves had also left the deer and came charging in to join the first two. Dad continued to call until the female was so close the .32-20 slug flipped her backward when it slammed into her neck. The other wolves slid to a halt, slipping as they turned to flee. Even at that age, Dad was a crack shot. He killed two more wolves, and his companion shot one.

And that's the way it started.

Dad did a lot of calling in his lifetime. Some of it was for sport, but much was out of necessity. He used the technique to kill pre dators that were preying on his turkeys, sheep, and goats, and he also provided the same service for his neighbors. Word eventually got around, and Dad's predator control techniques were much in demand. One time, hunting on a ranch literally overrun with foxes, he killed 105 in less than six hours. That year he got a total of 451. I'm confident no one has ever matched those records.

The first call that Winston and I made gave a fair imitation of the sound Dad made by sucking against his hand. The rabbit distress cry was the only sound we used for a long time. We had good success with foxes, coyotes, and bobcats, but weren't doing that well on raccoons. 'Coons are plentiful where I live, a few miles from Marble Falls, Texas, about 45 miles northwest of Austin. We couldn't figure why we couldn't call them consistently.

Then a freak thing happened. Seagulls migrate from the Gulf of Mexico to the reservoirs near Marble Falls. One day Winston and I were standing in my front yard when a gull flew into a high wire and fell to the ground.

The gull had a broken wing and started screeching. That got Winston and me thinking. 'Coons don't eat rats and rabbits, but

It doesn't look like much, but this is the first call my brother Winston and I made and sold. It copies the sounds Dad made with his lips. It's still on the market and popular with serious predator hunters.

they do kill and eat birds! Maybe that was it. If we could imitate those bird cries we might be able to up our average on 'coons.

Sometime after that we developed a bird call. But for the real test, I learned to make the cries by blowing on our Short-Range Predator Call and at the same time trilling my tongue against the rubber reed. Boy, did it work. We hunted on Lake Granite Shoals (since renamed Lake Lyndon B. Johnson) near Marble Falls, and we not only called 'coons—lots of 'coons—but we actually brought some near enough to scoop them up with a long-handled fisherman's landing net.

We made and sold a modest number of the short-range calls for two or three years, then decided we'd have to develop another call if we hoped for any repeat business. This one was made of wood with a copper reed, and we named it the Burnham Bros. Long-Range Predator Call. The first ones we shipped out came back promptly. The sound was lower than the high-pitched squeal of the short-range call and our customers didn't believe it would work; most even refused to try it. We switched to a brass reed to give it a higher pitch and it began selling. But we also found by adjusting the brass reed we could control the tone and pitch. Later, as callers became more knowledgeable, we intentionally made the tone lower to imitate a jackrabbit or a deer in distress.

Many callers don't realize that at a distance a call sounds higher pitched. Also, the sound of a lower-toned call reaches a longer distance, and I'm convinced it calls a wider variety of animals. A predator would rather ambush a half-grown jackrabbit, if available, than a cottontail because the jack is easier to catch. I ran a bunch of juvenile jacks down myself in my younger days, and if I can, you know a fox or coyote can. When I talk about calling, most people think about predators, but I'm convinced almost any animal—and many birds—can be called if we determine the sound that appeals to them. Most of what I've learned has been by trial and error. Some imagination doesn't hurt, either.

An animal or bird will come to a call because of distress, sex, food, or curiosity. You'd assume that distress and food go together, such as a rabbit's or bird's distress cries, but it's not necessarily true.

A friend once gave me a month-old red fox. I put the animal with some newborn kittens. When separated from the mama cat and kittens, the fox would cry, as all young cry for their mothers. That gave me an idea. Would the cries of a baby fox attract an adult fox? I made a recording of the baby fox's cries and it worked.

Our Mini-Call imitates the distress squeal of a baby gray fox. I got the idea years ago when I called two foxes and shot one, crippling the animal. The screaming fox was attacked by its own kind.

The more I thought about it, the more it made sense. I've seen another quail run to jump on a shot quail. When a calf gets hurt, other cattle will often rush it in a frenzy that appears to be sparked

There are several calls on the market that will imitate the seductive sounds of a hen turkey. Here a hunter uses a box call to bring out the gobbler—fanning in excitement.

by the bellowing of the youngster. For some reason these distress cries don't bring other animals to the rescue; they trigger exactly the opposite response.

The sex angle comes into play when calling species such as wild turkey, elk, moose, and deer. Yelping on a call in the spring fools a tom into thinking there is a lovesick hen willing and waiting. The whistling of an elk call makes a bull want to fight, to protect his territory and harem of cows. The bull comes to chase the intruder away and instead is ambushed by a hunter.

Yet I'm also convinced that many animals and birds are attracted to a call from simple curiosity, nothing else. When I'm trying to call coyotes in south Texas, using bird or rabbit distress cries, it isn't unusual to lure javelinas. I've brought them close enough to touch. I've also had jackrabbits and cottontails respond to a call, but I believe a rabbit comes only if it has a nest of little ones nearby.

In the case of javelinas, I just can't say for sure whether it's curiosity and only curiosity that brings them to a call. Researchers have noticed that javelinas occasionally kill and eat small rodents and wounded birds. I wouldn't be surprised if they raided a rabbit nest once in a while. But they aren't basically meat-eaters, so I guess probably they are more curious than hungry when they come to a call.

I've also had coyotes come in that seemed more curious than hungry. In fact, when I've made squeaking sounds with my mouth— sort of the way a coyote whimpers just before it howls—I've had other coyotes stand off and bark at me. A coyote isn't going to do that if it's hungry.

But knowing how sounds are developed isn't that important. Results are what counts. You must realize that the actual sound need not be perfect. No two turkeys sound alike, nor two rabbits, nor even two bull elk.

A California caller doesn't make the same dying-rabbit sounds as a Texas caller. The California caller puts more into it, more anguish in the sound. I suppose someone just started that style and others copied it. But the point is, the California caller and the Texas caller both get results. Where and how you call is much more important than the sound itself.

I don't believe a predator call that's tuned properly can be blown wrong. Most beginning callers don't blow loudly enough, but there's no sense in putting so much into the effort that you're winded in a couple of minutes. Take a deep breath, blow four or five times, pause to get your breath again, then call four or five more times. Just keep repeating this. You don't have to worry about the pauses; if an animal or bird hears the sound, it knows precisely where it's coming from.

One sharp-shinned hawk I remember was almost too precise, with instinctive "radar" that was as accurate as any of our sophisticated military missiles. It was early fall, a calm and cool morning. I was looking down a moderate-sized opening, the only direction I could see for any distance, and I was squeaking with my lips. The first series of squeaks brought a hawk into sight. It came streaking through the opening, directly at me. The flight speed was incredible and the hawk was on me before I had time to think. Subconsciously, I jerked my head to the side and the hawk zoomed past. If I hadn't dodged, I'm sure the hawk would have dug its talons into my face.

Such happenings are rare, however. With very few exceptions, when an animal or bird gets close to a human it'll spook, because it has either smelled or seen the intruder.

You don't want to be timid when calling. Many hunters call softly when game is close for fear of spooking the animal. The problem is, how do you know when anything's close? Your best bet is to go about your calling in a normal manner, loud at first, toning it down later. Call about 10 to 12 minutes for foxes, 10 to 30 for coyotes (they have super hearing and can come from a long distance), about 20 minutes for 'coons, and at least a half hour, maybe longer, for bobcats.

Some important advice is to treat every place you stop to call as though it's the only chance you'll get. Do everything to the best of your ability. Calling is a game of nerves and patience, and you'll need plenty of both. Don't hurry from one place to another. Take it in steps. I don't care how many predators are in the country you're hunting, you won't call one at every stop. Some animals won't respond, no matter what.

It's a never-ending learning process. I don't know how many times

I've called, but the number is in the thousands. I'm still learning. And I still make mistakes, like in the following incident.

It was February, along the Rio Grande out in the wilds of west Texas. It's big country. Brewster County's as big as Rhode Island and Connecticut combined. I've got a ranch on the river near Langtry. My neighbor came to visit me and said he'd found three sheep that had been killed the night before. Tracks told me three lions were the killers. Lions often come across the river from Mexico.

One track was exceptionally large, obviously made by an old male. I wanted that lion, so I began planning. In the sandy riverbed I found where the lions had been traveling regularly, through mes-

At 13 I was already hunting and had a trapline going, but even with experience going back this far, I'm still learning . . . and still making mistakes. The lion hunt described in this chapter is a good example.

quite trees and greasewood brush. After considerable scouting I selected this spot as the best place to ambush a lion.

In the daylight I picked a place to park and a path to walk. Shortly after nightfall my wife, Jolene, and I loaded up and drove to the river.

I made my first mistake before I left the house. I had two rifles, a .222 and a .308. I picked up the .222 only because it had a ring on the scope where I could attach a shooting light.

We walked quietly, not uttering a word, following the beam of a dim light pointed almost straight down. Getting into position, I started to call. Almost an hour later I gave up.

I knew the lions were traveling through this area, but the question was, When? The following day Jolene and I got up long before daylight and returned to the same place. We tried again and got the same results.

That afternoon we fished the Rio Grande for catfish until darkness tucked the rimrocks in. On an impulse I suggested to Jolene we try the spot one more time.

Another mistake; I was too casual about the whole thing. Maybe it was because I'd been concentrating on the fishing and not thinking about the hunt. I have to get a little bit excited to get serious—sort of like a football player psyching himself up for a game.

I'd been calling less than five minutes, turning my head to rotate the light. I never saw the critter coming. When I brought the light around, there they were, two eyes shining. Jolene and I had worked out a plan beforehand. I would rest the rifle across her shoulder to shoot and she would switch on the 12-volt light she was holding. When I saw those eyes, however, the plan started to unravel.

I knew it was a lion, but something told me to wait to be sure. A lion has eyes like no other predator, not even a bobcat. A bobcat's eyes are round and wide apart; those of a lion resemble deer or sheep eyes, green and sort of slanted. Maybe I hesitated because I thought it might be a deer. Frankly, I don't know why I did what I did.

I kept calling. It seemed like eternity, but probably was no more than a few minutes. The animal started walking, and now there was no doubt; the smooth, level movement of the eyes told me this was a lion.

Switching on my shooting light, I tracked the cat through the scrub mesquite and creosote bush. If I'd done my homework properly, I would've known the location of every tree, every bush. Then I would've known exactly where the lion would be in the open for a shot. And I surprised Jolene when I cut on the shooting light. She was expecting to feel the gun barrel touch her shoulder as a signal.

Jolene was fumbling with the sealed-beam light; it had a faulty switch. Finally, it flashed on. With the shooting light I couldn't get a good picture, but now I could see the lion plainly. He was about to disappear into heavy brush. With the disruptions, I was hurried to the point that I had to act instantly, almost in desperation. I fired and the lion spun and went down. But he was on his feet in seconds and disappeared into the night. Maybe I hit him too far back, but it seemed like a killing shot because the lion was bleeding from the first track on, a good blood trail. As I followed the animal, I was kicking myself for not bringing the .308.

The river sand was soft and damp from a shower and the lion was easy to follow. As we stayed after him, I dragged a stick in the sand, making a visible trail to follow out. Otherwise, I don't think we could've found our way through the thick brush at night.

We followed the trail for about 300 yards, but we still hadn't gone far from the place where we'd called because the cat was circling, almost to the point of cutting his own trail. I could tell he was dragging one leg.

I didn't like the way the lion was acting. It seemed the animal was trying to get behind us. This thick brush along the Rio Grande is no place to get in a cat-and-mouse game with a mountain lion. A wounded one is unpredictable and dangerous, and the track indicated this one was plenty big.

Jolene and I hurried back to the pickup and drove to a neighbor's, hoping to find a dog that would track the lion. The neighbor didn't own one, but he began calling other neighbors and friends. A couple of them had dogs, all right, but they didn't want to risk them on the trail of a crippled lion.

My intent was good, but it was another mistake to get that many people involved. Come daylight, ranchers from miles around converged on the spot.

I found the blood trail and could tell the cat was badly hurt. Periodically, through the night, he had crawled into thickets and piles of driftwood, each time leaving a large puddle of blood where he rested. All the people milling about pushed the cat to the river. I followed the trail to where the lion had jumped in. The Rio Grande is deep and swift here, and in February it was numbing cold. I knew the lion didn't have a chance in its weakened condition. He was swept downstream and drowned.

I was sick. If I'd been alone, trailing slowly and deliberately, always watching ahead, I'm convinced I could've slipped close enough to the lion for another shot. If I'd brought the .308 instead of the .222 I probably would have spent my time skinning a cougar rather than tracking one. See what I mean about still making mistakes?

Chapter 3

Electronics and Tapes

When Burnham Bros. went into the business of recording wildlife sounds, it opened up a whole new world. A mouth-blown call has certain limitations that dictate what you can or can't do. Recordings, on the other hand, have wider possibilities.

One example of a mouth-blown device is the Mini-Call, which imitates the distress cries of a baby gray fox, as I mentioned in the previous chapter. I carried that idea around with me for the longest time. I knew the sound I wanted, but I didn't know how to achieve it. I couldn't get the high-pitched frequency to make the correct sound with our standard calls and plastic, metal, and rubber reeds. Then one day I noticed some discarded pieces of magnetic recording tape laying on a table. On impulse, I picked up a piece, held it tight between both hands, and blew on it—and there it was, just the tone and pitch I was seeking!

You don't have this problem with actual recordings. You get what you hear. That's why I produce a wide assortment of cassettes and try to come up with two or three new ones each year.

You have three options for rebroadcasting these sounds. Phonograph records have the least going for them. They're bulky, difficult to carry around, and tend to scratch easily. With eight-track cartridges, you can put four different sounds on each tape and switch the sounds instantly by merely pushing a button. But the most versatile and economical method is the cassette player. With most

Carry a variety of tapes and if one sound isn't producing, try something else.

models, all you do is insert the proper cassette and you're in business; the built-in speaker gives adequate volume. But if you do need more volume, such as when calling crows, you can use an amplifier and an auxiliary speaker at the end of a 25- to 50-foot extension cord.

I like to use the auxiliary speaker when I photograph wildlife

The speaker can be set yards away from your position so there's less chance of detection.

because I can set it away from my position. When a fox or coyote is attracted to the distress cries, it runs toward the source—the speaker. There's less risk of the critter seeing me snapping pictures or hearing the camera shutter. I use an eight-track caller for my photographic sessions, because the tape keeps calling continuously. With a cassette, you might come to the end of the tape and have the machine shut off at the most critical time. I've called and photographed many animals while using only a mouth-blown call, but it's difficult to hold even our Short-Range Predator Call between the lips and blow while trying to concentrate on photography. That animal is homed in to your position and will notice every false move or unnatural sound, like a camera-shutter click.

This is why an electronic caller is to your advantage. Occasionally I get telephone calls from people who complain about electronic callers being prohibited in their states. I tell them these recordings are illegal only for hunting; you can use them to call animals and birds just for observation or for photography, or you can use them as instruction tapes, listening to the sounds and trying to imitate them with a mouth-blown call.

Personally, I think the notion that we can take advantage of animals by using electronics is nonsense. You might take advantage of them the first time, but certainly not after that. Wild creatures are much more crafty and adaptable than most of us realize. For instance, I can remember when poisons were widely used for killing coyotes. This method may have controlled them in some places, but it sure didn't eradicate them. In the part of Texas where I live, it seems a varmint hunter comes out from under every rock when fur prices are high. Yet the more varmints they kill, the more there seem to be the next year.

Properly managed hunting, even with the use of electronics, doesn't have much impact on animal or bird populations. Hunting is like pruning a tree; if the correct nutrients are there, the tree will come back stronger than ever. Animals and birds need a proper habitat and the right food. Climatic conditions have a much more dominant influence on wildlife populations than calling or hunting do. The proper food has to be available at the right time, too. The number of predators, for instance, may get larger or smaller, but only because of fluctuations in the number of rabbits and rodents, their primary food sources.

Another gripe of mine is the suggestion that those who record distress cries can only do so by harming or injuring animals and birds. Baloney! Animals and birds scream from fright, not pain. Catch a wild animal that's accustomed to roaming free, it'll holler.

When you're going after a bobcat you have to be patient, and continuous calling for a half-hour or longer is much easier with an electronic caller.

I remember the first tape I made of a baby cottontail rabbit. Cottontails like to build nests around barns, near other outbuildings, and along overgrown fence rows. I was a short distance behind my house, spraying weed killer along a fence, when suddenly out jumped three small rabbits. Recognizing an opportunity, I dropped the sprayer and ran to the house for my tape recorder.

I set up the recorder, switched it on, and picked up a baby rabbit in each hand. They began squealing. After about a minute, I set them onto the ground and they hopped off, right to their mama waiting nearby.

Another time I found a hole where a flicker woodpecker had cut through the wood siding of my house. Getting the recorder ready, I put a fisherman's landing net over the hole and banged on the wall. The woodpecker flew out—right into the net. I recorded its squeals, then turned it loose unharmed. The next day it was right back in its den.

But not all creatures have to be captured to be recorded. I had a couple of pet crows that stayed around the house, and all I had to do was put a cat where they could see it. You never heard such carrying on! I recorded the barking of a fox squirrel by getting into a pecan tree grove at daybreak and calling one close.

Just having a sound on tape isn't enough, however. It has to be the right kind of sound. For this reason I'm continually researching and experimenting.

I once surprised Russell Tinsley and George Fawcett with a new tape. I told them I had this "different" sound and I wanted to try it on "sound-shy" coyotes, meaning coyotes that had been called recently—the most difficult ones to fool. It's a rare coyote that makes the same mistake twice.

One cold, moonless January night we drove to a back pasture on George's ranch in south Texas. We went to a calling site I was familiar with and got everything set. I purposely swept the headlight across their faces when I switched the player on. I wanted to see their reactions.

I had to smile. Russell's and George's jaws both dropped when they heard the sound: a chicken squalling. I don't know what they'd expected, but it wasn't that!

There's more to the story, though. That night I used the tape to call three coyotes—in a place where I would have been satisfied to call only one.

How did I get that tape? Simple. After dark, I walked to the chicken house on my ranch and reached up and picked a bantam hen off the roost. The chicken probably thought a 'coon had her. She was so scared she screamed her head off—just the kind of distress cries that will appeal to a chicken-killing coyote or 'coon. This call was so obvious I don't know why I hadn't thought of it before. Others, though, aren't so obvious.

The distress cries of a baby 'coon come to mind. I am convinced that some predators prey on the young of other predators. My first experiment with this approach used a baby 'coon tape to call gray foxes. One night in springtime—when predators have their young— I drove down a county road close to my home, stopping periodically to call, just observing and not hunting. I stopped three times and called four foxes.

It's quite a thrill to see a coyote come charging toward you.

A tape of a deer bleating is good for calling coyotes, bobcats, and lions. Various bird distress cries—of woodpeckers, meadowlarks, and cardinals—are exceptionally good for 'coons, but they're also effective for just about every other predator. Baby javelina distress cries will bring in coyotes and bobcats, but will also attract javelinas. When a herd of javelinas hears this sound and thinks a baby's in trouble, they come with a mad on—the hair along their backs bristling and their teeth popping. They're spoiling for a fight.

This particular sound agitates them. It's like "different strokes for different folks"—different sounds appeal to different animals. You have to know what sound to use and where. That's part of what makes wildlife calling so fascinating, yet unpredictable. Every calling experience is unique.

Chapter 4

Camouflage, Decoys, Scents, and Other Aids

Back when we started in the game-calling business, Winston and I sort of muddled along with our country boy ways. We had a bunch of original ideas, but we didn't recognize them as such. For example, we would drive to a place in Austin that sold theatrical supplies and buy dark grease paint to camouflage our faces. As far as I know, we were the first to do that. But we didn't realize the potential of developing a grease paint to sell specifically to hunters. Somebody else beat us to it.

Even before that, however, we used our imaginations. We put mud packs on our faces, like women taking beauty treatments. Mud packs weren't as practical as grease paint or headnets, but they did the job. We also cut leafy branches to hold in front of our faces as we called. If we were heading to south Texas in the winter, when there was no available greenery, we'd cut cedar limbs at home and haul them from one calling spot to the next.

These two tricks, incidentally, dated back long before we got into the game-calling business. We learned the value of camouflaging our faces while stalking spooky ducks on our stock tanks—as ranch ponds are known in this part of the country. After we chased the ducks from one pond to another a few times, they really got sus-

I like to get in front of a bush rather than behind it; I'm hidden and I have good visibility.

picious and wild. That's when we had to start using our imaginations and improvising.

Another thing I learned as a kid is that you don't have to spend a lot of money to do a good hunting job. I was fortunate to be able to buy a few cartridges, much less anything else. I was more interested in the next meal than I was in a camouflage suit. (Anyway, camo clothing wasn't available back then, except maybe at an Army surplus store.)

I will admit that the stuff available today makes hunting a whole lot more pleasant and convenient. You can buy camouflage clothing suitable for shirt-sleeve weather or subzero cold. The olive-drab or dark-gray pants and shirts I wore as a kid doubled as hunting clothes and work clothes. I never imagined I'd see the day when I'd have camouflage suits to use for nothing but hunting.

But slipping into camouflage doesn't remove the challenge of hunting. Things like camo clothing, scents, decoys, binoculars, and scope sights are aids, nothing more. It's how you use them that counts. Successful hunting is based on preparation and skill.

Nowadays many different animal scents are on the market. My old standby is skunk scent. I've been depending on it longer than I can remember.

Years ago, Winston and I would either pack a dead skunk or squeeze its dark-yellow musk into a can. Imagine what we smelled like! But after some experimenting we discovered that we could place the carcass or can of musk downwind from our calling position.

When calling in the snow, wear white. In this instance my rifle should also have been wrapped in white.

If a predator tried to circle to pick up our scent, the stinky skunk would play tricks on the animal's nose and confuse it just long enough for one of us to get a shot. You can buy artificial skunk scent, but I'm sort of a traditionalist in that I like the real thing. I carry the malodorous liquid in a tightly sealed jar, however, and I'm very, very careful with it.

Whether or not I use a scent depends on the circumstances. Back when I used to do a lot more bowhunting than I do now, I depended a great deal on scents. If I didn't carry skunk musk, I'd use cedar oil scent, squirting it liberally on my stand and on clothing. I used this scent because most of my hunting was in country that had an abundance of cedars. I believe in using scents that are familiar to the animals. Using an apple scent wouldn't make much sense in my area since we don't raise apples in this part of Texas. I've scattered apples along with shelled yellow corn on the ground on my ranch and have had the deer eat the grain and ignore the apples, for whatever that's worth.

A young turkey gobbler can't understand what's with his plastic friend.

Any time you're going to have animals close, such as when you're calling or bowhunting, a scent can give you that little edge that makes the difference. I believe it's helped me while "horn-rattling" buck deer. I'll go into this technique in more detail later, but basically it's simply the practice of banging two antlers together to make a buck believe two other bucks are fighting. The buck rushes to the scene, either to whip the other combatants or to steal the doe away while the others are preoccupied.

A whitetail buck has a super sense of smell. When he comes to the sound, he might first try circling downwind. But if he smells a human, he isn't going to stick around to find out what's going on, so I use an unsealed jar of skunk musk. Some rattlers I know cut the urine-soaked hocks off a buck's hindlegs and carry these smelly pads around in a coffee can with a snap-on plastic top. Before they start rattling, they set the can down a few yards downwind and take the top off. The theory is that the rutting smell will not only mask human scent, but will actually help attract the buck.

Many scents are made from the urine of various animals. Does the urine of any animal have a distinctive smell that other animals can recognize? Beats me—I'm no expert on urine.

This coyote actually attacked the stuffed jackrabbit decoy.

Another hunter's aid is the decoy. Decoys are an integral part of waterfowl hunting. They've been around almost as long as the sport itself, so no one questions their use.

Yet, suggest the use of a decoy in spring-turkey hunting and some purists will throw their hands up in despair. I honestly can't see the difference between these two applications. Decoys add to the sport of waterfowl hunting, so why should the use of a decoy in turkey hunting seem like taking advantage? If you can come up with a logical answer, you're smarter than I.

I've heard the argument that decoys aren't needed in turkey hunting. That's true. I've also hunted ducks and geese without decoys. Whether it's used for hunting doves or waterfowl or even predators, a decoy only adds a different touch.

Yes, I've used decoys for predators, too. In particular, I've tried various types of decoys when calling coyotes. I like to watch a coyote's reaction when it sees the fake. I've draped a deer skin and a coyote skin—both crude decoys—over a bush, and I've had coyotes come right up to them to sniff. But the most effective decoy is a mounted jackrabbit. I've put the rabbit near the camouflaged auxiliary speaker of my tape player. When coyotes come to the rabbit squeals and sight the decoy, they actually rush to jump on it.

I've also used a stuffed doe while horn-rattling bucks, and I've seen an amorous buck try to mount the female. The confused animal couldn't understand why his lady friend toppled over! Some of my experiments have been amusing, and I recommend you try them if you want to have fun.

Using a decoy like this is the obvious application, but you're probably unaware of other uses. In the lowslung brush of south Texas, a man-made deer stand is a common sight. This is nothing more than a boxlike structure set atop legs and steadied with guy wires.

It doesn't take an old buck long to recognize the stand for what it is. A buck passing nearby will instinctively glance at the tower and immediately know if something out of the ordinary is there—such as the shape of a human. You know how I tricked one old buck? I put a dummy in my stand and left it there several weeks

The doe in the left foreground is stuffed; the buck behind is live. He came to the sound of rattled antlers.

prior to my hunt. When I replaced myself with the dummy, the buck didn't recognize the difference right away, and that was a fatal mistake.

I used to do the same thing when bowhunting on my ranch. Anyone who says a deer won't look up doesn't know what he's talking about. It seemed that whenever I climbed into a tree stand, the first deer that passed by noticed my presence and snorted to alarm every other deer within hearing distance.

I found a way to stop that, however, by hanging a pair of camo coveralls on my stand a month before the season opened. After that, when a deer came by, it didn't even glance up.

Years ago, I packed a lot more stuff than I do now. With experience you learn what you actually do and don't need. The lighter you travel, the better off you are.

Yet, some things are almost indispensable. If I'm hunting deer in strange country, I take a flashlight. I use it to get to my stand before daybreak—in fact, at least an hour before first light—to give

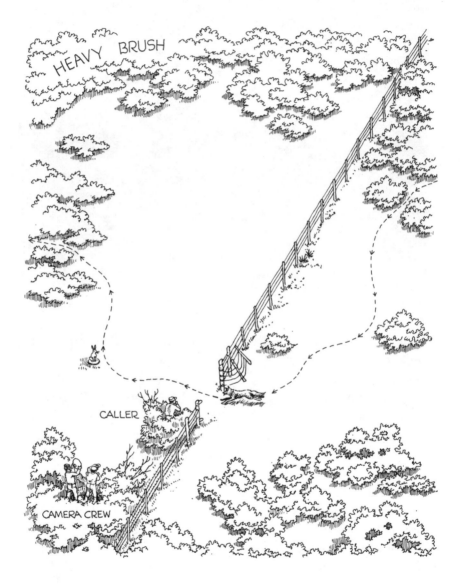

Predators, like humans, usually travel the path of least resistance, such as through this open gate. Open country also dictated where we put the jackrabbit decoy.

any deer that may have heard my approach time to settle down. And when I'm ready to quit, I don't get out of my stand until it's totally dark. Dad taught me that. If you leave your stand while there's any light left, you'll spook the deer, and they'll probably be suspicious of your stand from then on. But if you wait until full darkness to depart, you can slip away without alarming the animals.

A rifle scope sight is another must. I can't understand why anyone would buy an expensive rifle and not equip it with a sight of comparable quality. I want the very best scope sight money can buy. A scope sight will make you a better shot, no matter how good you are already. This is especially true early and late in the day or when you're hunting with a light at night. A quality scope not only magnifies, it also gathers and intensifies light, presenting a much better sight.

A common mistake is to use too strong a scope. Even when I use a 3 x 9X variable scope, in general I set it for no more than 4 power. The more powerful the scope, the more your shakes are magnified. At 9 power, it will seem that the crosshairs have a good case of buck fever, jumping all over the place.

The same is true of binoculars. When I'm big-game hunting, I'd rather leave my rifle at home than my fieldglasses. Many hunters think of binoculars as a tool for long-range hunting, such as for mule deer in the western mountains. They do the job there, of course, but they also serve a role when you're hunting the thick underbrush where whitetails hang out. With binoculars, you can see into places where unaided vision can't distinguish shape from shadow. But, again, don't make the mistake of letting someone talk you into binoculars that are too powerful. It's hard to beat 7 x 35 glasses for all-around use. The first number indicates the power, the second the size in millimeters of the front (objective) lens. A large front lens only adds bulk and weight. In most hunting situations a smaller size won't make any difference because large objective lenses, such as 50mm, add little or nothing in performance until it is almost dark. Any power greater than 7 only makes it that much more difficult to hold the glasses steady. If excessive power makes your vision shaky and blurry, however, binoculars will probably be more of a hindrance than a help.

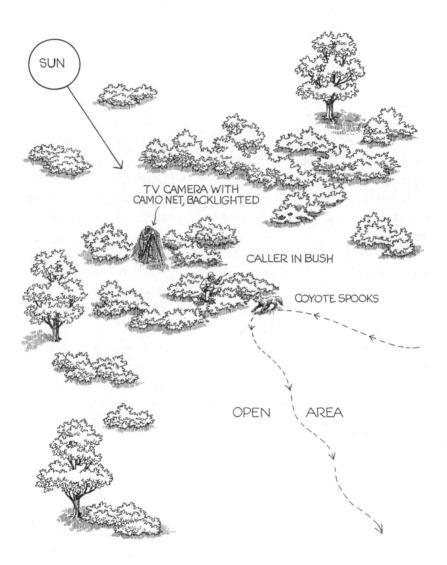

Little things make the difference. I thought this was a good setup, but the coyote was spooked when sunshine hit the cameraman, who was covered with mesh camo cloth. He should have been positioned in front of a bush.

One more bit of advice: consider binoculars a long-range investment and buy the very best pair you can afford. Cheapie glasses are not as sharp and if the parallax is off even slightly, you'll end up with a headache. Quality glasses are super sharp and distortion free.

One piece of equipment I've always been fussy about is my footwear. Tennis shoes are quiet and comfortable if it isn't too cold, but me, I've always worn hunting boots. Leather is superior to any synthetic substitute. It costs more, but it's worth it. I'm speaking about the boot itself, not the sole. Leather's actually the worst choice for soles because it's hard, slick, and noisy. My favorite was a crepe sole. It was real spongy and quiet, but it wasn't durable and didn't last long. I guess that's why boot manufacturers quit using it. Now I just use a rubber sole. It's quieter than anything else available.

When you get a pair of boots, be sure they fit comfortably and break them in before you go hunting. I've seen hunters go to Colorado with new boots, and they were crippled after the first day. Flat ground is bad enough, but up-and-down mountain terrain really puts stress on your feet.

As for clothing, dress for the worst possible weather conditions. You can always take clothing off, but you can't put more on if you haven't brought it with you. When I went to Alaska in late winter to hunt wolves, I had no idea what to expect. So I asked my host, Dick Hemmen of Fairbanks, what to bring. Thanks to him, I was reasonably comfortable when I could have been miserable or maybe even frozen to death.

If you're going into an unfamiliar environment, don't be afraid to ask what to bring. Suppose you've booked an elk-hunting trip to Wyoming and you've never hunted there before. Ask the outfitter what you should bring. You'll avoid a lot of problems that way.

One problem I've tried to avoid is excess weight. Just the weight of a rifle is tiring, and if you're also wearing binoculars around your neck, you don't need any extra baggage, like a big sheath knife flopping about on your hip. I use a knife only for gutting or skinning an animal, and an ordinary pocketknife is plenty adequate for either of those jobs. I also carry a pocket stone to keep it sharp.

If I'm after big game, such as elk or moose, I carry a small saw in a belt sheath. The saw is lighter than a comparably sized knife, and it does a better job of slicing through bone and muscle.

I carry items, like the belt saw, fresh flashlight batteries, spare calls, and an extra honing stone in what I call my "hunting bag," which is actually an airline flight bag. After years of adding and discarding items, I've pretty much limited the contents of the bag to the essentials. When I'm ready to go hunting, I toss the bag into the pickup and don't have to worry about leaving something behind.

One "must" is any prescribed medication, such as blood pressure pills. I've never found a drugstore out in the woods. If you take medication and can get an extra supply, put it in the bag and never take it out. If you can't get spare medication to put in the bag, clip a note to the handle. When you pick up the bag, the note will remind you to bring your medication.

The same is true of prescription eyeglasses or contact lenses. You never know when you might break your glasses or lose a lens. And the bag certainly should include basic first-aid supplies, including aspirin.

One time, Russell Tinsley, Bruce Brady, and I went on a deer-hunting trip to south Texas. We had miserable winter weather—rainy and cold. After we'd been there a day, Russell came down with the flu. We had two alternatives: either break camp and head home, or try to keep Russell alive for the next couple of days so Bruce and I could hunt. Thanks to the hunting bag, I had a large bottle of aspirin. Somehow Russell survived and Bruce and I both got nice bucks.

Along the way you'll learn what to add to your hunting bag. As I dig through my bag, I notice a length of parachute cord, boot waterproofing, extra laces, spare flashlight bulbs, a camo headnet, waterproof matches, an extra knife, a sharpening stone, a couple of spoons and a can opener. These are the kinds of essentials I often forget when packing. My hunting bag acts like insurance.

I usually put the bag behind the seat of my pickup so there's no chance of driving off and leaving it at home. But no plan is perfect.

Once, as I was heading for a hunting trip to south Texas, I discovered that my pickup wasn't hitting on all cylinders, so I went back home and borrowed Jolene's car. And yes, you guessed it. When I got to the ranch where I intended to hunt for several days, I remembered the bag—back in Marble Falls in the pickup.

Maybe I should try tying a string around my finger.

Chapter 5

Calling Foxes

One point I always stress with beginning callers is never to underestimate the quarry. I remember one fellow I took out. At the first stop, in less than five minutes, I called a gray fox. It rushed in close.

"A gray fox sure is dumb," he told me later.

"It might start out dumb," I replied, "but it wises up fast."

I quit calling any wild animal dumb long ago. A young one might be naive, but it doesn't take it long to get wise to the facts of life.

I've learned this from calling and observing thousands of foxes. You can learn much more about an animal by calling and observing it than you can by calling and shooting it. The more you learn about the behavioral patterns of an animal like the fox, the better hunter you become.

I was too young to remember when I first started going with Dad on calling excursions, but by the time I was 10 I was hunting by myself and at age 13 I had my own trap line. I vividly recall an incident that occurred when I was 10 years old. One reason I remember it is because it was probably the most bizarre incident I have ever experienced or seen.

People didn't travel much back then because they lacked adequate means of transportation. As an alternative, kinfolk who lived near one another visited frequently. One day my mother's sister, Aunt Freda Michel, came to visit and told Dad a fox was getting her

The fox raced in, jumped over the rock, and clamped down on Dad's wrist.

chickens. The hens had young chicks and were free ranging, so they were easy prey for foxes. Except for an occasional handout of grain, chickens at that time had to hustle their own food. They roosted in trees or wherever they could get up high. We didn't lock them up at night in chicken houses.

Dad told Aunt Freda he would take care of her problem. It was nearing daylight when we stopped the car near her house on the Colorado River of Texas, not far from where I now live. We walked maybe a half mile into the rocks and cedars. This is rough country.

Dad positioned me behind a rock and hid by another nearby. He was wearing a dark gray workshirt, which was almost perfect camouflage; he appeared to be part of the rock. Putting his double-barreled shotgun over the rock, he cocked both hammers, ready to shoot. This would save a split second if the fox appeared.

Dad began lip squeaking. He'd been calling only a few minutes when suddenly it happened. Before either of us even saw it, the eager fox sprinted between us, jumped onto the rock, and bit Dad's wrist. The instant the fox grabbed hold, it let out a squall. Why, I don't know. Dad jerked to get loose and one barrel of the shotgun went off.

Jumping up, Dad gave another hard shake and got rid of the fox, which ran off. Dad grabbed the shotgun and fired the last round, hitting the fox in the rump but not killing it. The animal got away.

His arm was bleeding profusely, so we hurried to town to get a doctor to treat and bandage the bite. Because the fox had escaped, Dad had to start taking a series of rabies shots.

But, would you believe, while taking the rabies shots, Dad went back to practically the same place several days later, called the same fox, and killed it? He knew it was the same animal because it had a broken tail and pellets in its rump.

The story doesn't end there. Dad's wound festered and wouldn't heal. One day, he took the point of a knife blade, dug in the wound, and found one of the fox's molar teeth—what you might call a tusk—embedded in his arm. It had broken off when the fox had bitten him. I would find all this hard to believe if I hadn't been there.

Foxes are widespread, fairly plentiful, and not too difficult to call. The gray fox is easier to call than the red only because you can predict its range better. The red fox likes open country and is like the coyote in that it roams a lot. But if a red fox is within hearing distance of your call, you're going to get its attention. A fox is a fox.

I've always said that a fox can be hard to hit with a bullet because there's so much space around it. The animal's size is deceptive. Its pelt makes it appear larger than it really is. A gray fox weighs about eight to 11 pounds, and a red fox weighs six to 15 pounds.

While the gray fox likes woods and brushy areas, the red fox prefers more open country. Their behavior differs in other ways, too. The gray fox is an expert tree climber, while the red rarely climbs. Gray foxes maintain dens all year long, while reds use dens only to raise their young. A red fox has great stamina and can run for miles, but when a gray fox is pressed, it races into a crevice or up a tree. Since the gray tends to stay in a more limited area, it aggressively defends its territory from the intrusion of other foxes. When the range of the two fox species overlaps, the gray fox usually predominates.

In their true colors, it's easy to distinguish these foxes, although some southerners refer to the gray fox as a "red fox" because it has a little bit of reddish hair alongside the gray. And while the true coloration of the red fox is a rich, burnished orange-red, many color variations can be seen across the country. But one quick way to identify a fox is to look at the tip of the tail. A red fox's tail is always white tipped, while the gray's tail is black tipped.

As with all wild animals, a new crop of foxes comes along every year. By late summer the spring-born are able to hustle for themselves. There's no telling how many young slicktailed foxes I've called close enough to touch.

But calling foxes from late summer on into the fall just for observing and practice can present a problem later on. These may be the same animals you'll be trying to call and shoot in the wintertime. Early calling might make them call shy.

What I do is use two different sounds, or "change the tune," as I call it. I let the foxes hear one sound early on, then give them something different in the winter. This difference might be nothing more than a change in pitch if I'm using rabbit distress cries: a high-

Every animal, such as this red fox, is an individual, and you can't predict how it will react to a call.

pitched call early on, and a coarser or deeper tone later. With an electronic player, you might use entirely different sounds, such as a rabbit squeal first, then bird distress cries. Much of your success in calling will depend on your imagination.

Even if electronic callers are illegal where you hunt, I recommend that you get a selection of live animal and bird tapes and listen to them to become familiar with the distress cries you're trying to achieve. Many articles about game calling describe a deep-toned call as a "jackrabbit model." That's inaccurate. The sound is actually closer to an imitation of a half-grown jackrabbit, which isn't much different from an adult cottontail.

If you call a fox and then spook it, perhaps by shooting, it'll usually associate that particular sound with danger from then on. I'm convinced that predators have much better memories than we give them credit for having.

Every once in awhile, however, you'll run into an exception. One time Winston and I were calling on the coastal plain of south Texas near Port Lavaca. The terrain consists of salt flats sprinkled with heavy cedar brakes. It was early morning, not yet sunrise, when a fox came to our call. We shot at it with a bow and arrow, but the arrow only nipped its hindleg. The fox ran off, so we moved about a half mile and called again. Another fox came, and we killed it. To our surprise, it was the same fox with the telltale freshly bloodied leg.

What made this fox do what it did? My theory is that if you don't shoot at an animal with a gun, you really don't frighten it all that much. I don't believe we frightened the fox when we nicked it with the arrow. There was no loud sound for the fox to associate with danger.

This fox came to lip squeaking, the call I learned from Dad. This is the call I make by squeaking with my lips, with my hand over my mouth to regulate the tone and pitch. I move my hand back and forth—sort of like a trumpet player putting his hand over the end of his horn—to vary the sound. The technique really isn't that difficult, but at first you might have trouble creating a sound. It takes some practice. Swallow saliva until your mouth seems abnormally dry. With your mouth slightly open, roll your lips back between the teeth and start sucking air gently without biting down very hard. Just keep at it until squeaks begin coming from one side of your mouth. The secret is to use the reservoir of air within your mouth; you don't want to gulp air, because the idea is to keep the lips slightly compressed. You don't force the sound; it has to come naturally and with little effort.

This photo of me calling a gray fox close has been used in many of our magazine ads.

But this is only one of many sounds I habitually use. Foxes will respond to a wide variety of sounds. My Burnham Bros. Long-Range Predator Call with rabbit distress cries is a long-time favorite. I also like mouse squeaks, bird distress cries, and our Mini-Call with its fox distress squeals.

With electronic calling you have an even wider choice: lip or hand squeaking or rabbit distress cries; various birds like the wood-pecker, meadowlark, or cardinal; fox distress cries; baby house cat distress cries; or chicken squalling. And any sound that will call a fox will call other predators like coyotes and bobcats, no matter what you've heard to the contrary.

If you pick one sound and have success with it, that's fine. But the more sounds you can imitate—or the more tapes you have for your electronic caller—the better off you'll be because you can change the tune, as I mentioned earlier.

To give some inkling as to what this advantage means, J. D.

Taylor and I were once calling near Colorado City in north-central Texas. J. D. has been a hunting companion of mine for many years, and he's a first-rate caller. It was a cold and clear January night on a ranch with an abundance of fox signs. But, in a way, these signs were misleading. Deer hunters had been calling foxes and a government trapper had been calling and trapping them, so they'd been under lots of pressure. J. D. and I made several stops before we eventually called one.

We brought this fox in with a tape of a half-grown jackrabbit. The gray fox was nervous, running in and out. I took a snap shot and missed as it went around a bush. The fox ran into the night and disappeared.

Immediately I pulled a Mini-Call from my coat pocket and began blowing on it. The eight-track player was still going, and I was getting a mixture of jackrabbit and fox distress cries. In less than a minute, the fox came back from the same direction it had run off in, and this time I got it.

Another time, J. D. and I took turns calling. He was using his favorite tapes: half-grown jackrabbit and woodpecker distress cries. I was using house cat distress cries. J. D. had recently hunted the same ranch with the same tapes and the foxes were wise to the sounds, but they'd apparently never heard the house cat cries. I was the only one to call foxes that night, which should tell you something about the importance of changing the tune.

But the calling sound must be put in its proper perspective. Unless you're calling where foxes are, it makes no difference what sound you use because you won't be able to call anything. Throughout this book I'll keep repeating the importance of scouting.

Learn to read sign. I look primarily for droppings, which are easy to find along livestock and game trails or country roads. Foxes are a lot like humans; they travel the easiest routes. You can't depend much on tracks because they're almost impossible to find. A fox doesn't weigh much and the ground has to be damp, soft, or powderlike to reveal a track. Even so, it's difficult to tell how fresh the tracks are.

That isn't the case with droppings. Also, the distribution and number of droppings give good clues as to the fox population. You can examine the droppings and tell what the foxes have been eating. If the dung is dark with hair or bits of feathers, the fox has been eating meat—bloody stuff, rodents, rabbits, or birds. This tells you to try the more open, grassy areas at night when rodents and rabbits are foraging. Predators go to the food sources.

Foxes are not entirely carnivorous. They'll eat all sorts of wild berries, fruit, and even grasses; they'll take advantage of whatever is available. But in the winter, their diet is pretty much limited to small animals and rodents.

If possible, I prefer to call in places where there's no livestock. Domestic stock is in competition with wildlife. Without livestock, there's more ground cover, which means more rodents and rabbits and thus more predators. You might draw a comparison with a lake that has black bass. If the cover is removed, small prey fish can't reproduce and multiply in number. So available food disappears and so do the bass.

While you're scouting for sign, select places where you'll call later. This way you can go directly to the spots with as little disturbance as possible. Try to figure where the animals will be at any given time. Early and late in the day, call close to rough country or brushy areas where foxes den and hide. Try to speculate as to the direction from which you expect animals to come and what direction the wind will be blowing and pick your calling spot accordingly. Have some open country downwind of your position where you can see anything approaching.

I like to hunt straight into the wind or with a quartering breeze, depending on the lay of the land. This means I travel from one calling site to another into the wind, straight or quartering. I don't want to let the cautious animals know I'm coming.

If I'm in hilly or timbered country, I move about a quarter mile between stops. Even in more open terrain I go no more than a half mile. If you're not careful, you'll travel past foxes. Then when you get set, the breeze will carry your scent back to them. When you're not moving very far between stops, there's no need to call real loudly. A fox can hear even a moderately loud call for some distance.

I think a light breeze is better than a calm—no wind at all. The wind covers your sounds as you move about, yet it doesn't hinder successful calling.

Some callers fret too much about the weather conditions. If a gusty wind is blowing you might as well stay at home. Otherwise, do the best you can. It's important to believe in yourself. If you stay with it and do everything to the best of your ability, eventually you'll call one or several foxes.

If night calling is permitted in your state, try it. Foxes are nocturnal prowlers. They're out looking for something to eat, and that makes them easier to call.

But the countryside looks entirely different at night, so it's doubly important to do your homework. Pinpoint potential calling sites during the day and mark them so you can find them after nightfall. I spend three or four hours in the afternoon just getting the hunt organized. I stack rocks, make markers from sticks, or drape white tissue on bushes or branches to indicate the calling sites I've picked. I use tissue paper because it soon disintegrates. Rags are litter, and if you leave trash lying around, you'll wear out your welcome with the landowner.

When I select a site, I examine it thoroughly in the daylight. I want to have a mental picture of every bush, tree, and opening. This way I know when to turn on a bright light at night to get a clear shot. I also pick a place to park and a path to follow. I leave as little to chance as possible. I even carry a hand axe and clippers to remove any obstructing limbs or bushes. I don't like any distractions.

When I head to my calling site at darkness, I drive with only the dim illumination of my parking lights, if possible. I don't like to flash headlights through the woods. Even if the light doesn't frighten foxes, it'll make them suspicious. When I park I put the front end of the vehicle into a bush to obscure the grill. On a moonlit or starlit night the chrome will shine.

I use a red light, or what I call a "no-scare" light, which I'll describe more fully in the chapter on night calling. When I get into position, I switch on the headlight and commence calling, rotating the light to look all about. With all the exercise I've had, I probably have the most limber neck of anybody.

I once read that a caller recommended calling for a minute before turning on the light. Do you realize how far a speedy fox can travel in less than a minute? He also said you should switch on the light for a minute, then turn it off for a minute, alternating on and off. When someone asks me about that, I question how can they see in the dark. Most of them never thought of that. I want the light on the whole time I'm calling. A fox can appear at any time. I would guess that more foxes show during the first five minutes of calling than at any other time.

With a red-lens light you don't even have to be really careful about keeping the beam off the ground. But you can also call the critters with a conventional white light. Just keep it dim and aim it up off the ground. The faint glow around the beam is sufficient for spotting eyes. For shooting, I like a bright shooting light mounted right on the gun. You can switch it on when you're ready to fire.

A moonless night is best for calling foxes. You can call them when there's a moon, but you need to stand in the shadow of a tree or squat by a bush. Otherwise, the animal can detect your silhouette. Also, the added illumination of the moon makes it more difficult to see eyes. You almost have to sweep the beam right along the ground to pick up the glow.

When you pick up oncoming eyes, let the fox get as close as possible before making your play. But if it starts to turn sideways, you'd better shoot right away because the fox is beginning to circle to get the wind. If it scents you it'll take off a lot quicker than it appeared.

At night, things can be deceptive, always looking farther away than they are. If you're using a shotgun, it pays to pace off the distance to various landmarks. This way you'll know exactly when the fox is within effective killing range. I'll go into more detail about the guns and shotshells for this hunting in the chapter on firearms.

If you call continually, the fox is likely to rush in. When it bounces into view, get your gun up and be ready to shoot the moment you switch on the shooting light, whether it's mounted on the gun or being operated by a companion. It's impossible to predict how the animal will react to the sudden brilliance. It might hang around briefly, or it could take right off.

Many times you can sort of regulate how fast the animal comes to your call by the way you call. Constant calling brings the animal in more rapidly. On-and-off calling makes it react more deliberately. Blow a few distress squeals, wait a minute or two, then blow briefly again. Spend more time looking than calling. I like to call this way when taking photographs. A fox that comes more deliberately usually stays around longer. But with on-and-off calling, there's a premium on sitting motionless and being quiet. One advantage of constant calling is that the sound covers human error.

Normally a fox will react negatively to an unnatural sound. More than once, I've taken another person calling who'd sight a fox and say, in a loud voice, "Here it comes!" What he should have said is, "There it goes!"

If you call a fox fairly promptly—within the first five minutes—and you shoot it, simply leave the animal where it falls and continue to call. That fox might have company since they sometimes travel in pairs. But don't stay put too long; 12 minutes is the maximum. You'll be better off trying a fresh place than staying there any longer.

There's an exception to this rule, however. If your hunting country is limited, stay in one place a little longer. You don't have anything to lose. You might pull in a fox from a long distance, maybe from the neighbor's place across the fence. I've had a fox come after 25 minutes of constant calling, but this is a rare occurrence.

Actually, I like to travel the perimeter of the area, calling near fences and bringing foxes out of neighboring ranches. This way I can get maximum utilization of my calling country.

If visibility is good, I prefer to stay on the ground to call. But if need be I'll climb to the low fork of a tree to see better. Foxes don't seem to care much whether the sound originates from the ground or from a slight elevation. But if I'm using an electronic caller I'll put the speaker on the ground. That way the fox homes in on the sound source and I, sitting above the ground, can move into shooting position without the animal knowing I'm there.

Many callers call constantly because they fear an animal won't be able to locate the sound. Forget that worry! Once a fox hears the call, it knows precisely where it is originating.

My friend Lynn Willis can tell you exactly how precisely foxes can locate sounds. He was sitting in a tree stand with a bow and arrow, waiting for deer. After a spell of seeing nothing, he became bored and decided to do some calling. He took a call from the pocket of his camouflage shirt and began blowing on it.

Almost before he knew what was happening, an eager gray fox was in the tree with him. A gray fox can climb a tree like a squirrel. The fox actually got on the same limb with Lynn, too close for a shot with bow and arrow.

Lynn didn't know what the fox's intentions were, and he didn't want to find out. He hollered and kicked at the fox and the animal took off.

And Lynn decided he'd had about all the excitement he could stand for one day.

Chapter 6

Duping a Coyote

The opportunity for calling a coyote never has been better. This animal continues to multiply and expand its range. The coyote both fascinates and amazes me. It can adapt to almost any terrain and climate, from the desert to thick timber to open plains, dry conditions or wet. I've hunted these animals many times on Padre Island, which stretches for about 100 miles along the lower Texas coast. Coyotes seem to be right at home among the grass-topped sand dunes. I've seen them wading and looking for fish and crabs. A coyote can learn to eat almost anything. It's a master of survival.

Lord knows, man has tried his very best to eradicate the coyote, using everything from traps to poisons. In most instances, this effort has been pretty futile. Actually, I believe man probably has done more to encourage the expansion of coyotes than he has to discourage it. He has unintentionally created a superior breed of coyote by encouraging selective breeding, just as race horses come from the best blood lines.

Man's eradication efforts have killed the dumb coyotes, leaving only those a cut above the crowd to reproduce. Through generations, we've created a supercreative animal that can and does live within seeing distance of skylines of some of the largest cities. It learns to get by, eating whatever it can find, which sometimes includes small family pets like dogs and cats.

Some people hate the coyote, but others admire it. In either case, you can't help but be fascinated by this animal and at least tender it grudging respect.

As for the coyote's adaptability, consider these three documented examples: An Oklahoma bitch coyote got about on two hindlegs, having lost both forefeet. A male shot near Fort Stockton in west Texas had a heavy steel trap clamped to one of his legs. The trap obviously had been there for many months, which made it almost impossible for the usually nimble critter to catch natural food. Biologists speculated the coyote had subsided on carrion found along the highways. A California female, although completely blind, was fat and healthy and even managed to raise a litter of pups.

Yet still another factor for the coyote's rise and spread is the animal's unique personality. Harry A. Goodwin of the U.S. Fish and Wildlife Service once observed that the coyote "is one of the most aggressive and successful competitors with man for the same habitat."

Many people mistake these doglike animals for wolves. True, a coyote in New England doesn't resemble the slimmer specimen found in deep south Texas, but this can be explained by environment. Dr. Raymond Coppinger of Hampshire College in Amherst, Massachusetts, studied the Eastern coyote and wrote that "anatomical characteristics change readily when animals move into new regions."

But there is suspicion that coyotes migrating east of the Mississippi River had some interbreeding with domestic dogs in their backgrounds. If true, this might explain why some Southern coyotes—with their doglike, blunt noses and shaggy fur—weigh 50 pounds or more, while in the Western open spaces 30 pounds is exceptionally large for a coyote.

Civilization is another factor that can't be ignored when discussing the coyote's persistent territorial spread. Man, through ecological changes, has reduced or eliminated available food, scattering these animals in their search for something to eat. Tagged coyotes have been captured more than 100 miles from points where they originally were trapped and marked.

One knowledgeable field representative of the Fish and Wildlife Service once admitted that we can only expect to control the coyote population, not eliminate it, even with modern technology. The truth is, the coyote is too slick for humans. Since it is virtually impossible to exterminate coyotes that inhabit only a small area, once the survivors are left alone, they quickly build the population again. Coyotes sometimes have exceptionally large litters—15 or 16 pups—and parents are very protective of their offspring, assuring a high survival rate.

I mention this only because I want you to be aware what kind of animal you're confronting. I've tricked more than my share of coyotes, and I have had more than that trick me. A coyote is quick to detect any human mistakes. I guarantee, it's one of the sharpest animals in the woods.

It's also one of the most nervous, perpetually on the move. A coyote leaves an abundance of tracks and droppings. The animal will trot along a trail or country road, or through the edge of a clearing instead of back in the brush, and around the perimeter of

Can you immediately spot the coyote in this photo? The animal is more difficult to see than you might expect.

a waterhole if the shoreline isn't muddy. One thing you'll notice while scouting is that all coyotes will water at one spot at a pond instead of at random. This place will be nearest the most convenient escape cover. Yet such a spot isn't very good for calling. An animal like the coyote is most alert and edgy at a waterhole because it feels threatened. Predators often wait to ambush their prey near water.

Another unusual thing about the coyote is that it'll leave droppings at any leak, no matter how slight, in a gas pipeline. The odor put into natural gas for some reason makes coyotes want to relieve themselves right there. In south Texas, where I hunt frequently, this is the way pipeline leaks are located—searching for an abnormally large amount of coyote droppings in a small area.

Look for tracks, which resemble those of a dog, and fresh droppings to determine where coyotes are traveling. They'll pass this way again some time of night or day. If a coyote's within hearing distance of your call, it'll come to you.

If you have a choice of day or night calling, I recommend you try calling during the day first. If you hunt coyotes at night you'll make them vehicle shy, light shy, scent shy, and human shy—all at the same time.

A funny thing about the coyote is that it might be suspicious, not coming in to your call, but it nevertheless is curious. Once you get up and leave, it'll cautiously approach the area and sniff around, to see what's been there.

One time Winston and I were hunting with Stanley Clayton near Pearsall in south Texas. This ranch obviously had some supersharp coyotes. We couldn't call one into the open. They'd just hang back in the brush and bark at us.

But we outslicked the critters, or at least one of them. After several tries with no success, we told Stan what we intended to do. We left him hidden while Winston and I got up and walked back to the pickup, making all the natural noises like talking and slamming the vehicle's doors, to let the coyotes know we'd left. About a half-hour later we came back and found that Stan had shot a big dog coyote. He told us that shortly after we'd left, here came the coyote, nose down, sniffing the trail, following exactly the way we'd gone.

A young coyote, naturally curious and naive, is not difficult to call.

A coyote will come readily to a call during the day. During the winter, you might call one at any time, even right around noon. In my country, I like a light northeasterly wind overriding moist air coming up from the Gulf of Mexico to make a light mist or fog. Coyotes will be traveling all day long. They're on the prowl, and they'll respond to a call.

At other times of the year, you'll probably do better early and late in the day, with early probably being the better choice because you usually won't have as much wind. But I've called coyotes at the height of the day, even in the summer.

I did this on the hunt I took with Wally Taber near Laredo on the Mexico-Texas border. Wally makes a tour with his popular safari show in the winter, so filming is limited to other times of the year. He wanted to do a sequence on coyote calling, and the only time we could get together was August. In south Texas, you can fry an egg on the hot ground during that time of year. But we called coyotes, lots of coyotes.

Camouflage is important when you're calling predators, but this is doubly true with coyotes. You can't overdo it. I completely cover my body, including a mesh headnet and camo gloves. Some people dislike the headnet, saying it gets in the way and obscures their vision. It won't if you go about it the right way. Put the net over your face and have someone help you cut eye and mouth holes. Later, when you get ready to call, draw the net into place, then put on your cap or hat and pull it down firmly, to anchor the headnet into place. I've found the net to be quicker and more convenient than grease paint, and once you get used to it, it's no bother at all.

But even with proper camouflage, you still have to sit quietly and motionless. A coyote is quick to detect anything unnatural. In all my years of calling and photographing coyotes, I've seen only one that was not spooked by the sound of a camera shutter. That was a mature, prime coyote I called in the wintertime. Remarkably, of the thousands I've called, that coyote was the only one not spooked, which will give you some idea of the coyote's paranoia.

As for stifling movement, it's obvious that you must move if you intend to shoot the coyote. The key is to move at the right time, when the animal's vision is blocked. But if you have eye contact with the animal, don't even twitch. The coyote has eyesight like you can't believe.

And if you move, be cautious and don't make any noise. As I said before, even the almost inaudible click of a camera shutter will make a coyote jump with fright.

Then there's the matter of a prevailing breeze. Be aware of the wind direction at all times. Let it dictate your movements. A whiff of human scent is one danger signal that no coyote ignores.

For calling, I prefer a coarser call, one deeper in pitch and tone. I often use the Burnham Bros. Deer Call. I think the deeper-pitched call works on a wider variety of animals and is easier to blow.

For electronic calling, my old standbys are lip squeaks as well as half-grown jackrabbit, house cat, and woodpecker distress cries. If the coyotes are smart, I use a tape of lip squeaks mixed with fox growls, or a mix of house cat and fox distress cries. I've used mixed sounds for most of my calling career because often they'll get results when one type of distress cry won't. Way back, Winston and I used to dupe coyotes by blowing calls simultaneously. I also like to blow calls while a tape is playing. It really works. One of my favorites is an adult cottontail or half-grown jackrabbit tape playing while I chime in with lip squeaks. Or you might want to try a predator call with a rabbit tape.

Although scouting before calling is a definite plus, sometimes I have to hit a place cold, improvising as I go along. If I'm in country where the coyotes are familiar with vehicle sounds—and in most places they're accustomed to at least infrequent travel—I drive around until I locate a likely looking spot, then simply put the pickup into reverse and back up until I find a place to hide the vehicle. I don't gun the motor; I make the move as unobtrusive as I can. After I've parked, I walk back to the spot I've picked to call.

Night calling is the same for coyotes as for foxes; select your places during the day and mark them. One of the myths floating about is that coyotes can't be called at night. Bunk! I've called no telling how many, as far back as I can remember.

The place you choose for calling is critical. Ideally, it should be away from any timber, with bushes few and far between. You want to have a good field of view. If a coyote is going to come to a call, it won't hesitate to cross or come into more open country-side.

But sometime you might have to call in timber or thick brush because you have no other choice. A coyote will respond even in this type of country, but it'll appear and disappear quicker in tight quarters. You might have only a fleeting chance for a shot. Under these circumstances you're probably better off using a shotgun (see the chapter on guns). You might spend some time practicing night shooting with a shotgun, because it's different from day shooting. Two factors that change are time and distance in tight quarters. You have to merely point the gun instinctively at night, rather than aiming; it's more snap shooting than anything.

In open country you're better off with a rifle. For night hunting use a scope sight with a shooting light mounted on it (our light mounts on a ring clamped on the scope). Since shots might be on

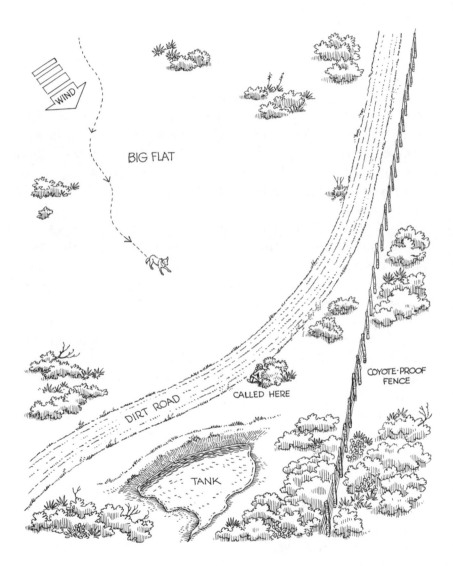

I chose this position because I had good visibility into the wind and didn't have to watch my backside because of the man-made barrier, a wire-mesh fence.

out yonder, consider a powerful shooting light, like a 12-volt, sealed-beam lamp.

I'd rather control the shooting light than depend on someone else. The problem with your partner handling the light is that he can't see oncoming eyes unless he's in line with your hunting headlight. He doesn't know when to switch on the shooting light, nor where to point it.

Sometimes I'm the light man, with both the red-lens headlight and shooting light, while my partner is the shooter. Before starting to call, I make sure he knows and understands my signal to tell him when to shoot. When I rotate the headlight and pick up eyes, I hold the beam slightly above and in front of the animal. I prefer a light with a red or orange lens, but you can use a white light if it's held right—above the animal where the beam won't hit its eyes. When I think the coyote is within shooting range, I waggle my headlight back and forth two or three times to tell my companion to get set, that I'm getting ready to switch on the shooting light.

One trick I've learned is that if you have a coyote or other predator approaching in a sort of circular movement, you can bring it closer with manipulation of the headlight. Train the beam slightly in front of and above the eyes. A suspicious animal like the coyote doesn't seem to want to cross the light, so it will angle toward you rather than cutting the beam.

Another thing about the coyote is that one animal learns from another. If you're in an area where all the animals are coming from the same direction, the first one will dictate the pattern. For instance, one might be coming to the call when it sees or hears something suspicious and flares away. The next coyote will pick up this one's trail and follow it exactly. It won't come any closer than the first one did. However, for some strange reason, if they're coming from many directions, this won't be true. They'll cut each other's trails and not seem to pay any attention.

But even on the best of days, you might not have many chances. It's important to make the first shot count. When Pete Brown was shooting editor of *Sports Afield*, he showed me how to gain a bit of advantage. At the time, we were hunting in Mexico. Winston and I used to go to Mexico four or five times each year to call. The

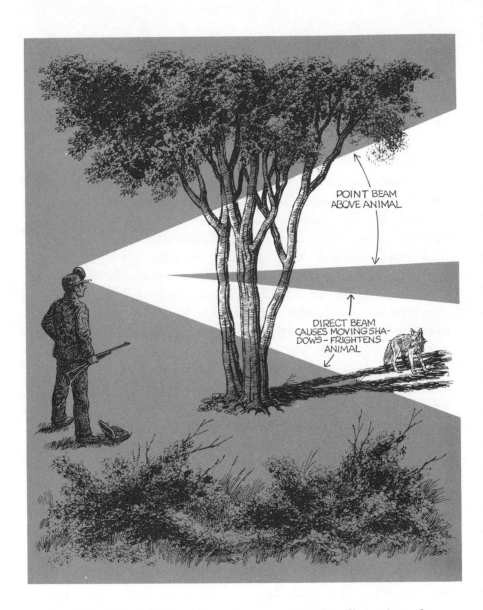

Within the image: POINT BEAM ABOVE ANIMAL

DIRECT BEAM CAUSES MOVING SHA-DOWS — FRIGHTENS ANIMAL

A headlight beam flashing through trees and brush will spook predators like the coyote; that's why you want to keep the beam above the animal's normal line of sight.

marshy, salt-flat country about 100 miles below Brownsville, Texas, near the Gulf of Mexico, was literally loaded with coyotes.

When I would pull a coyote into open country with my calling, Pete would raise his rifle. It would seem like eternity before he finally squeezed the trigger. But most times that he shot, the coyote would go down. Pete taught me that you don't have to panic and hurry. You've usually got more time than you think you do. You might have to rush, all right, but it's a controlled rush. That first shot probably is going to be the only good chance you get. If you fire and miss, the frightened coyote is going to shift into high gear.

I learned a lot about coyotes during those many years of hunting in Mexico. One thing I learned is there's no sure thing when it comes to matching wits with coyotes. Winston and I were on a huge cattle ranch where we knew there were coyotes. We found ample sign and could hear them yowling just at twilight. Also, we knew no one else had been calling there, but the coyotes were ignoring our calls. We finally figured out why. The rancher often would drive around in his pickup with his two dogs—a greyhound and a cross between a Doberman pinscher and Afghan hound. When he sighted a coyote crossing open country he would turn the dogs loose. The greyhound would run the critter down and the big crossbreed would kill it.

After this kind of harassment, the coyotes soon learned to stay out of open country. The coyotes probably were hanging back in the thick brush. When Winston and I got back in the heavy cover, we had no problem calling coyotes.

If you do much calling, you'll run into different situations like this. You have to use some common sense and try to figure why the coyotes' behavior is erratic or there's no response to your calling. Sometimes you'll come up with the right answer and sometimes you won't. On some trips you won't call anything, just as you don't catch fish every time you go fishing, even in the best of places. Accept it and try again. It's all part of the game.

Chapter 7

The Mysterious Bobcat

I get letters and telephone calls regularly from callers and would-be callers. From the questions they ask, I know the bobcat is the biggest mystery to most callers. They think the cat's smart, but it's not. Calling a bobcat is no more difficult than calling any other varmint. All you have to do is locate one, then give it time to come to your call. A hunter's impatience is the bobcat's best ally.

But though the bobcat's not mysterious, it's certainly unpredictable. You never know how one will react.

Consider one winter night when Winston, Russell Tinsley, and I were hunting near Sweetwater in northcentral Texas. There are lots of cats in that area, and I wanted Russell to get one, because he'd never shot a bobcat.

But I never expected one quite so quick.

It was late January and the landscape was leafless and bleak. There was no wind and a cold, fine mist was falling. The weather was miserable, and soon we were damp and chilled.

Shortly after dark, I drove to a place where I'd found much bobcat sign. We three climbed into the pickup bed and got ready and I started calling, swinging my light around. The first sweep caught eyes. They were coming double time. The animal was so eager, I figured it was a fox.

The critter ran right to the pickup before I could aim my light on it. To my surprise, it was not a fox but rather a long and lean bobcat. It was looking up into the light and its tail was twitching.

Russell later said the cat was so close he couldn't find it in the rifle scope. Instead of aiming, he merely stuck the muzzle within inches of the bobcat's head and pulled the trigger and that was that.

I guess if I hadn't stopped the bobcat by aiming the light on it, the animal would have gone on by, under the pickup. With the extralarge tires, there was ample clearance.

In about three hours of calling, we brought in four more cats and Russell killed two. These four came to the call in a more conventional manner than the first—slow and deliberate. That first eager-beaver had me puzzled, however. But maybe I solved the mystery the next morning when I opened the cat and examined its innards. It was full of stomach worms. The bobcat was probably slowly

I called this lanky lynx in Alaska.

starving to death and just the promise of a meal brought it on the dead run.

Compare that with another cat I called while this book was in preparation. I'd called for a full 45 minutes before it put in an appearance. See what I mean about bobcats being unpredictable?

I must admit that for a long time bobcats were a mystery to me, too. Then one summer Winston and I dedicated ourselves to getting some action movies of bobcats coming to a call. We called 55 cats during daylight in about a month's time. Several times we had as many as three in sight at once. That summer cram course taught me a lot about bobcats.

For one thing, I learned that calling a bobcat is sort of like getting your first deer with bow and arrow. It seems like an impossible assignment, but after you get that first one, it's no longer a big deal. Self-confidence has as much to do with it as anything.

I've talked to people who've spent much of their lifetimes in the woods, yet have never seen a bobcat. Bobcats are nocturnal and furtive. You seldom see one roaming around, even if you live where there are a good many cats. I'm convinced that there are a lot more bobcats than most people think.

Bobcats range from about 15 to 20 pounds, and any tom larger than 30 is a rare trophy. While the bobcat is a relative of the Canadian lynx, the two inhabit different geographical regions, and the lynx is larger and more silverish in color. But the lynx, like the bobcat, will respond to a predator call.

To call one, you have to hunt where they are. With apologies, I have to mention scouting again. Do your homework. Look for tracks and droppings along stream banks, brushy washes, and waterholes. A cat's different from a fox or coyote in that during the day it travels through thick cover. That's why you seldom see one. But at night it roams around freely in search of something to eat.

That something to eat is primarily rabbits, rats, and mice. The staple diet will be whatever is predominant. Texas A&M University researchers studied bobcats in Kleberg County of south Texas. The stomach contents of 125 bobcats were examined over a two-year period. The first year, when cottontail rabbit and cotton rat numbers were down, the cats preyed on 21 different species. The second year, when rabbit and rat populations rebounded, bobcats fed on

A cat is difficult to see when it's among rocks.

these small mammals to the exclusion of almost all other prey. But a similar Arkansas study revealed a larger proportion of rats and mice in the diet than in the Texas study. While the bobcat's selective, it's also like humans in that it's an opportunistic predator; it takes what's most available and easily caught.

My favorite bobcat-getter is our Deer Call. My second choice is the Long-Range Predator Call, the model made from walnut, not plastic. It has a deeper tone.

When you start, blow fairly loudly. After about 15 minutes, you can let up to a softer, easier blowing pattern. You don't have to do anything fancy, just make it repetitious, the same call over and over. Check your watch and stay with it for at least a half hour. A cat often takes its own good time in coming.

In fact, during the daytime a bobcat might come and go without your ever knowing it was near. I've had many bobcats pull this trickery on me, but I recall one incident in particular. Winston and I were calling not far from the town of Dove Creek in southwestern Colorado. This is real rough, rocky country. It was December and the countryside was covered with a light snow.

We were calling near a line of junipers. Although we'd found considerable bobcat sign, more than 30 minutes of continuous calling produced nothing. After we'd finished calling, I decided to circle and look. Footprints in the snow told the story. A pair of cats had walked through the junipers and squatted when they'd gotten close. The depressions made by their rumps were clearly visible. And another line of tracks showed how they'd left. Winston and I had no idea those cats were anywhere around.

A bobcat sometimes behaves that way, squatting behind a bush and just listening and looking. It might come closer and it might not.

Many callers believe that when a cat squats, that's as close as it'll come. Not necessarily. I remember one cat that disproved that theory.

Winston and I were calling near Eagle Pass on the Texas-Mexico boundary. From all indications, this ranch had very few varmints— a few coyotes and even fewer bobcats. We must have called at least a dozen times over a two-day period before we finally got a cat to show.

This one was 60 or 70 yards away when it squatted in a clearing. It just sat there motionless and stared. If I hadn't seen it come up and squat down, I would've sworn it was a statue.

Winston and I were well hidden, so we decided to play with this cat and try to make it come closer. I know exactly how long it took because I kept checking my wristwatch. After 35 minutes of squatting, the cat got up and continued walking toward us, showing no fear. By the time it stopped a second time, either Winston or I could have reached out and touched it.

Only now and then will a cat squat down in the open like that, however. It often stays in cover or behind a bush. It pays to use binoculars when trying to call during the day. Fieldglasses let you look much more thoroughly. Sometimes the glint of an eye or a movement will give the cat away; the stubby tail seems to be continually twitching.

If you've ever watched a house cat stalking its prey, you can get a good idea of how a bobcat usually comes to a call, sneaking furtively from one bush to another. And when it eventually squats down, if you didn't see it coming, you might look right at it and not realize what it is. The bobcat has a good natural camouflage and it isn't going to move.

Another time I was hunting in south Texas with Roy Esse. It was an overcast, dimly lit day. It's usually easier to see a bobcat in these conditions than in bright sunshine. I was glancing back and forth as I called when I saw something in a clearing about 50 yards away. It stopped my roving eye because it was something that wasn't there before. I had to look for a few seconds before I realized it was a bobcat. How it got there and squatted without my seeing it, I don't know.

But a cat can be deceptive. Winston and I were once calling in north Mexico, across the Rio Grande from Del Rio on the Mexico side. I was looking at a sun-parched clearing that was as bare as the carpet in your den. Near the center of the opening was one small clump of grass. After nearly 30 minutes of calling, I brought a bobcat from the nearby brush. It walked through the clearing and disappeared behind the grass clump not more than 30 yards away. There didn't seem to be enough cover to hide the cat, much less let it make good its escape. But that's what happened. I never

I sat along a pasture road and pulled this cat out of the brush.

saw the bobcat leave, never saw it again. It was almost as though it had vanished into thin air.

Because the bobcat tends to be sneaky, it pays to call where you can get a little bit of elevation so you can look down into the ground cover and have better visibility. Hunt a place where the brush is at least scattered so the bobcat will have to cross an opening. Many callers bring up bobcats they never see; the animals quietly come and go.

One way to eliminate the sneaking is to use a nonfood call with your electronic player—such as house cat distress cries instead of rabbit or bird distress cries. I don't know why the bobcat comes to this particular sound unless it's just curious. But this tape is one of the best for attracting cats.

Some other sounds I've found super effective are lip (hand) squeaks, woodpecker and cottontail distress cries, and a mountain lion's mating call, a weird-sounding mixture of screaming, growling, and yowling. This sound really does produce.

With a cassette, I like the same sound on both sides. When one side finishes, all you have to do is flip it over. Let one side play completely before you move. You should stay in one place at least a half hour, maybe longer, when after bobcats.

A mistake even with a small portable cassette player is to turn it up too loudly. There is no need for that much volume. Turn it to about half volume. A predator can hear it for a long, long way.

One time I was trying out a new tape on George Fawcett's ranch in south Texas. I've hunted on this ranch numerous times. I turned on the tape of house cat distress cries and before too long, here came George's dogs. I was hunting exactly one measured mile from George's house and the dogs had heard the tape at that distance.

How far a bobcat will come is anyone's guess. But since it often takes a half hour for a cat to show, I would imagine it might come a long way. Sometimes they approach within seeing distance, then squat to look, then keep on coming close. As I said, a bobcat's totally unpredictable.

Larry Helms will tell you how close a cat can come. He was calling south of Fort Worth when he brought a cat up close and didn't even see it. Instead, he felt it. The cat had come in from the side and when Larry moved his hand, the bobcat swatted it. I suppose it thought the movement was a rabbit. The sharp claw laid Larry's finger open as though it'd been cut with a knife.

Where it's legal, I like to call bobcats at night. You can see the glow of a cat's eyes even in heavy brush, making it difficult for the animal to sneak close without your knowing it's there. The eyes of a bobcat are different from any other predator. They're wide apart and bright, probably brighter than those of any other varmint. And when a bobcat moves, its eyes sort of glide along in a smooth plane. A coyote's or fox's eyes tend to bounce up and down. A raccoon has eyes that somewhat resemble those of a bobcat's and you might be fooled by an oncoming 'coon until the animal gets close. But because of its unusual gait, a 'coon's eyes also sort of bob rather than glide.

A bobcat isn't particularly light shy, so you can use a white light, although I prefer a red or orange beam. As I mentioned in the chapter on foxes, a moonless night is best. If there's even a partial moon, a bobcat can see you unless you're hidden. And with the added light, it's more difficult to pick up the cat's eyes, unless you have the beam right on the ground. I especially like to hunt when the moon goes down late in the night. I sleep until about midnight, then go calling. It's uncommonly quiet at this time; the cats are prowling and seem to be less suspicious.

A bobcat depends more on its ears and eyes than it does its nose for detecting danger. Its sense of smell is only average, but it has superior hearing and eyesight.

The bobcat's eyes are truly remarkable. For one thing they adjust for acute night vision. The pupil narrows to a thin slit in bright sunlight, then opens in the dark to nearly fill the iris and intensify what little light there is, similar to coated optics in quality binoculars. The eyes shine brightly in a light because of a thin layer of light-reflecting cells, which gives the bobcat better depth-of-field vision than other predators. This means it can readily distinguish between what it sees in the foreground and what is in the background. And finally, bobcats can perceive things in fine detail because their eyes have an abundant supply of both rod and cone cells. The rods are sensitive to weak light, improving night vision, and the cones let the cat view the whole scene in exact detail. Sometimes just a blinking of the eyes or the movement of a shoulder will give a caller away.

With regard for the bobcat's eyesight and the ears—its ear tufts seem to have something to do with well-developed hearing, tests have shown—the caller has to remain hidden and quiet. One mistake can scuttle the entire operation. When a cat spooks, that's it. Once it leaves, I don't believe you can talk it back.

If you're camouflaged, hidden, and not moving, a bobcat might come close even from downwind. I've seen instances where I know a cat must have been able to smell me, but the critter just kept coming.

Don't make the mistake of ignoring your downwind side. When calling cats, watch in all directions. Otherwise, you might be in for a surprise as Bill McReynolds was.

I've had callers tell me they've heard bobcats squall. From my experience, what these callers hear is the squall of a hawk. The raptor often squalls at a call, but I can understand how a person can be fooled.

Bill was. He'd never heard that shrill noise before. We were calling in early morning below Cotulla in south Texas. I was blowing on a call and Bill was sitting in a brush clump and looking around. Suddenly, he was startled by a squall right behind him. He turned to look, downwind, and there, almost eyeball to eyeball, stood a bobcat. Miraculously, when Bill's head whipped about, the critter didn't move. I guess it was too surprised. But Bill did have the presence to swing his rifle around and shoot the cat in the throat.

That wasn't the first time Bill McReynolds had been shocked by a bobcat. Another incident occurred when Bill, Winston, and I were on a daytime call near Tilden in the south Texas brush country. We looked around until we located a likely place to try. It happened to be where there was a deer stand, a small platform about 10 feet high in the fork of a mesquite tree.

We suggested to Bill that he climb up and sit in the deer stand to get a better view. Winston and I would remain on the ground and do the calling. If a bobcat showed, Bill would be in position to shoot it.

A cat was closer than we thought. I held Bill's rifle as he scrambled up the tree. When he got near the wooden platform, he threw his hand on it to grab hold and pull himself up. But when his hand came down, it plopped against the side of a sleeping cat—and all hell broke loose!

The alarmed bobcat jumped off the platform, so frightened that it didn't land on its feet but rather hit awkwardly on its side and slid in a cloud of dust. Bill fell back and came out of the tree about as fast as the bobcat. He didn't land on his feet, either.

Chapter 8

Outsmart a 'Coon

Raccoons are pretty much all over and they're plentiful, so the prospects of calling one or more are excellent. And when you do get one to respond, it'll come close. A 'coon doesn't show much fear or suspicion. Many times I've had to holler and kick to keep one from climbing up my leg.

When I think about a 'coon approaching close, I think of Chris Burgess. He and I were driving toward the house on my ranch in west Texas when we sighted this rangy, long-legged 'coon crossing the road through the illumination of the pickup headlights.

"Let's get that 'coon," I said to Chris. "He's prowling around and he ought to be easy to call."

We were about a half mile from my house. We drove there as rapidly as we could over the rough road and got our calling stuff and walked back a few hundred yards toward where we'd seen the raccoon. We traveled slowly because in this country you respect the vegetation; almost everything has thorns.

This is wild and woolly terrain. Deep-cut dry washes spill off the rimrocks to the Rio Grande. When we get infrequent rain it's usually a downpour, and these washes become torrents. You don't want to be in one when a wall of water comes down.

The country is mostly rock held together by a little soil. Even a jackrabbit has to hustle to make a living. I've often wondered how a 'coon manages to survive, but this part of west Texas has a whole

Winston and I called many 'coons close enough to catch them with a fisherman's landing net.

bunch of these animals. And they're as mischievous as 'coons in other regions of the country. I inherited some chickens compliments of the fellow who sold me the ranch. They didn't last long. 'Coons got them, one by one.

Anyway, when I figured we'd walked far enough, I asked Chris to sit on a livestock salt trough. When he got settled and ready, I began blowing on the Deer Call, my old favorite. And in less than 10 minutes I got results.

The eyes were coming double-time. I figured it was a fox. I had only enough time to kick Chris to let him know something was on the way. By then I could see with my headlight that it was the 'coon and it was only 20 yards away. Before Chris could find it in the scope sight of the .22WRF Magnum rifle, the 'coon was standing between his legs and looking up at him. Chris did all he could do. He pushed the gun's muzzle against the critter's head and pulled the trigger.

Since a 'coon comes straight in and close and doesn't bounce around like a nervous fox, old black-mask makes for sporty calling using a bow and arrow. I've shot many with a bow. The only problem is that a 'coon sometimes gets too close and you wish you had a spear.

If you call one, keep trying. It might have company. Many times I've stood in one place and called several 'coons.

Not always are they as cooperative as they were for Willie Esse, Jr., and his brother Roy, however. We were calling at night near a large stock tank a few miles from Encinal in south Texas. In less than 20 minutes I called five raccoons. They came parading past in single file. Maybe I shouldn't tell this, but Willie and Roy shot at all five and didn't hit a one.

Although 'coons are night prowlers, you can call them during the day. During the winter, I like to call them early or late on a cloudy, misty day. I get into the heavy timber or the underbrush along a stream or near rocky outcroppings, anywhere 'coons might be bedded while it's daylight.

A 'coon isn't as alert to human scent as is a fox or coyote. It won't try to circle downwind. Its eyesight is about average as wild animals go, but it has super hearing. You don't want to make any unnatural noise as you call.

After nightfall, a 'coon is out looking for something to eat and it's easily fooled by a call. You don't even need an artificial light source. I've called many 'coons by using nothing more than natural moonlight. It's easy to see the dark blob of an oncoming 'coon, especially in the winter when the frost-killed grass is pale in color.

Look for 'coon tracks around streams and waterholes.

If I'm hunting with a light, I prefer no moon because it's easier to sight eyes with a headlight in total darkness. A white light will do, but I prefer a red or orange beam because you can be a little sloppier with your technique and get away with it.

You'd expect a 'coon to be smarter than that, considering its personality. A 'coon can figure things out. Dr. K. L. Michels of Purdue

University once did a study that proved a 'coon is smarter than a cat. 'Coons took only 800 first trials to achieve 75 percent success on just the second trial of a given problem. Cats, meanwhile, needed 7000 trials to reach the same peak of efficiency.

But I didn't need the good professor to tell me that. I have a chicken house, and anyone who raises chickens in 'coon country knows there is no keeping the 'coon out. If it can't undo the door latch, it'll claw the back wire or tin roofing to gain entrance. A 'coon is a destructive killer. Once the raider is going about its business, the only recourse is to either call it or trap it, and neither is an easy assignment. A chicken-house thief has mastered all the tricks.

When scouting for places to call raccoons, look first around water, a stream or pond. A 'coon is going to go where the food is. Other possibilities are around chicken houses, orchards, barns, and grain-fields. The best time to sucker one is during what I call the hungry season, in the winter when rations are slim. When there's plentiful food, I've experienced times when I could walk along at night and headlight 'coon eyes and try calling and the animal would show no interest at all. But if it's hungry, here it comes!

For mouth calling, try a 'coon call, deer call, or short-range predator call. I've had good success with all three. With electronics, play any bird distress or baby 'coon distress cries, or lip squeaks.

Call a little bit longer than you would if you were after foxes. A raccoon is a slower traveler. The natural waddling gait isn't as fast as the lope of a fox. Give a 'coon about 20 minutes, maybe a little longer.

If you're driving around at night and you see a 'coon, go past it a ways, park, and slowly and quietly walk back in that direction until you figure you're reasonably close to where you sighted the animal. You can call the 'coon most every time.

If I'm hunting at night with a partner, it's important that we communicate and know what to do in various situations. Charley Helms and I thought we had our teamwork well planned, but it didn't work out that way at first. We were night calling in the winter near Eagle Pass on the Texas-Mexico border. After calling for per-

Charley Helms and I teamed up to get these 'coons and a ringtail cat while hunting at night.

haps 15 minutes, I saw three sets of eyes moving our way. I waggled the headlight beam to tell Charley to get ready. When one 'coon got close, I switched on my hand-held bright light and dropped the beam on the animal. The trouble was, the beam also picked up another 'coon about 10 feet beyond the one I had spotted. Charley saw the back 'coon in the dimmer part of the light. He'd borrowed my rifle and the scope sight wasn't adjusted to his eyes. Charley fired and missed.

After botching that attempt, we regrouped, profiting from our mistakes. In two nights of calling we got 10 'coons, and after that first misfire, we didn't miss another one.

Incidentally, since 'coons come straight and close at night, you might be better off with a shotgun. But as I mentioned in an earlier chapter, practice shooting at night. It's different from shooting during the day.

When calling 'coons you might sometimes call a badger, if you're in country where this animal lives. Badgers and raccoons react in much the same way to a call, although badgers don't seem to respond as consistently. But like 'coons, they'll approach close and usually hang around for a spell. To call a badger I think you need to be near its den. I've called many with a deer call, but when one gets within sight you have to change to squeaking if you want it to stick around. It doesn't seem to like the lower-toned call at close quarters.

Chapter 9

Lions and Crafty Cats

One thing I've learned about cats: While the bobcat and mountain lion are kin, they're entirely different animals when it comes to habits and behavior. The bobcat has a limited territory, while the lion is a wanderer. It might cover 10 or more miles in a night. This wanderlust makes the cougar difficult to predict. A fresh track might indicate that the lion will travel that way again, but it could be days later. Calling a mountain lion is a hit-or-miss proposition unless you find a fresh kill. The killer will keep returning until the prey is eaten or the carcass starts rotting and stinking. In the wintertime a kill will remain edible for a longer time. But the problem is locating a kill. To do so you almost have to live in cougar country, unless you have others on the lookout.

A few years back, my friend Ray in Fort Davis in west Texas telephoned to tell me he thought he'd located a lion—no kill, but plenty of fresh tracks. I dropped everything and drove the more than 300 miles from my home.

In the afternoon we walked about two miles to where Ray had found the tracks. We had to walk since there were no roads. This is rough country.

We waited for darkness to settle over the countryside. It was a moonless night. When the time seemed right, I switched on my headlight and commenced blowing on the Deer Call.

In about 20 minutes the light picked up eyes—or an eye, I should

93

say. I never saw the animal coming straight on. When I first saw it, the lion already had turned sideways and my light reflected only one eye. Since then I've learned that when a lion gets close and sees or hears something suspicious, it'll turn. If your light is shining on only one eye, you'd better shoot, because the lion is leaving. That's what happened that night. The lion got away before I knew what was happening.

A cougar doesn't always act that way, however. Like its cousin the bobcat, it's unpredictable. Another time, my son Hunter and I drove to west Texas southeast of Alpine—really wild country. Hunter went in one direction to call, and I went in another. We figured this would double our chances of success.

The plan almost worked. A lion came to Hunter's call but was more casual than the other lion. It approached to within an estimated 65 yards and squatted down, looking and listening. Hunter was nervous enough as it was. He had only a nine-volt shooting light— not powerful enough to push the beam out to the cat. The animal was only faintly illuminated. Hunter couldn't see much through the scope of his .270 rifle, and he missed. If he'd had a powerful 12-volt light, I'm confident he would have gotten that cat. Hunter's a good shot.

While a lion can cover the miles, I'm convinced the available food supply determines how far it'll travel. If there's plenty to eat, it'll hang around.

I didn't know for sure, but I always suspected an American mountain lion and an African lion were similar in their habits. It was my dream to find out. By saving every extra dollar we could, Winston and I finally were able to afford a trip to Uganda. But I don't want you to confuse this with a safari. Winston and I had a missionary friend in Africa and he arranged a vehicle for us. After that we were on our own, a do-it-yourself sort of hunt. We learned as we went along.

We certainly learned about lions. I've never been real apprehensive when it comes to calling nature's killers, but I must admit that my first encounter with African lions was hard on the nerves. Frankly, for a short time there, I was scared.

This mountain lion track is identical in shape, but smaller than that of an African lion.

Carrying only a movie camera, Winston and I walked to a rock outcropping in a large grassy plain. The terrain was uneven, with scattered draws, trees, and thorn bushes. One reason we selected this particular spot was for security. We wanted elevation to see anything that might come through the tall grass. It was a good idea because lions don't have any natural enemies except man, and Winston and I neither looked nor sounded like man. We were in full camouflage and blowing on a Deer Call with its coarse tone. The two lions that came toward us were not afraid of us at all.

And that was the problem.

We hadn't picked the spot merely because it looked good. As with any hunting, we'd spent some time scouting. We'd found many fresh tracks in a dry river bed, so we'd picked a nearby location to, hopefully, make our movie. It was a good choice.

We'd been calling perhaps 20 minutes when we saw them coming, a pair of lionesses. They were putting the stalk on us, legs slightly bent, bellies down, as they slipped through the grass. When they

This African lion is one animal I called that actually frightened me.

got within 100 yards, one decided to come on in, straight at us, while the other began to circle. I'd seen wildlife movies of lions teaming like this to ambush their quarry. One moves in while the other waits in case the prey tries to escape.

The oncoming lioness would take a few quick steps, then stop and look, never taking her eyes off us. The other continued to circle. That's when I began to get a bit uneasy. But Winston and I were busy filming and there was really no time to be scared until later. Then it dawned on me what might have happened. The oncoming lioness approached to within 50 yards. If she'd decided to attack, she could've been on us—just that quick.

Winston and I finally decided it was time to surrender. We started jumping up and down and yelling as loud as we could. The lion didn't run. She simply stood there unhappy about the turn of events, reluctant to leave. Finally she turned and casually walked off and we breathed a sigh of relief.

Later, we got a big male. I wished we could have called him, but it didn't work out that way. We could hear him roaring through the night. From after midnight until dawn, we lay awake and listened. You could tell by the lion's voice that he was a large male and wasn't far off. But sound can fool you. We thought the lion was farther away than he really was.

At first light we jumped into the Land Rover and drove in the direction of the sound. We got too close—we saw him and he saw us. He trotted off, disappearing behind a bush. We drove on a short distance and there he stood, no more than 75 yards away. Winston shot him in the throat.

But maybe if we'd called the lion, we wouldn't have gotten him. It might have turned out the same as it did for Virginia Kraft in Nepal. Virginia is a writer for *Sports Illustrated*. She was put in a platform blind in a tree to watch for a Bengal tiger. After she got into position she decided to amuse herself by blowing on a short-range predator call. She'd been calling only a brief time when she glanced down and there, not 30 yards distant, stood a gigantic tiger. Virginia told me she was so petrified that she couldn't shoot. Shortly

I got this leopard while hunting in Uganda.

thereafter, the tiger turned and walked away. Later she killed a tiger by other means, but the one she called left a lasting impression.

Any wild cat, I'm convinced, can be called. On a hunt with Wally Taber, I called a rare and small margay cat in Mexico. Once while on a bear hunt in Ontario, I tried calling a Canadian lynx, just to satisfy myself that it could be done.

It could.

In Africa, the first time we called, we brought in a serval cat, similar in appearance to an American mountain lion. This one also had about the same coloration.

What was surprising was the variety of African game we called. We called a whole bunch of jackals. One would come in like an eager coyote. It was like a coyote in other ways, too. If we let a jackal get downwind of us, it would promptly spook and run. I wondered about that. With little or no hunting pressure, there was no reason for it to be so frightened of human scent, unless it was pure instinct, an inborn fear.

The jackal is an African animal that is easily called.

We called several different members of the antelope family, using the deer call and the short-range predator call. They came on the dead run like a whitetail doe reacts in my part of the country when she has young. I suspect the deer thinks whatever is making the noise is a threat to her fawns. Perhaps it's the same thing with African game.

From my personal observation, mama antelope has to be protective. African antelope are sort of like our rabbits; both natives and predators prey on them. They sure don't die of old age and they don't go to waste.

We also called some natives. They would hear the strange noise and they knew something was in heap big trouble, but they didn't know what it was. They would creep close to look and when a native popped from the brush, you could see the fright on his face.

That trip to Africa was educational, but it only supported a long-time theory of mine that predator calling will work most anyplace on all kinds of wildlife. I've corresponded worldwide with hunters who've called about any kind of game you can think of. From personal experience I sure know it works on those big killer wolves and wolverines in Alaska. It's just a matter of adapting to the country you're hunting and the animals you're after.

Chapter 10

Night Calling

Dad did a lot of calling, day and night. No matter what he was doing, he was mining new ground. He was far ahead of his time. Much of what I know I learned from him, but I've also had to learn a lot on my own. Maybe it's pure cussedness, but when someone tells me something, I don't accept it as gospel. I have to find out for myself.

Like calling coyotes at night. Back when I first got into the calling business, the general belief was that coyotes can't be called after dark. I can sort of understand how that myth got started. Unless you know what you're doing, you can't call them at night.

One mistake is to get in heavy brush instead of open country. I have a theory that light flashing through a bush or tree creates dancing shadows—an illusion of movement—that spook coyotes. Also, reflections off nearby bushes and trees let a coyote make out your shape. It only takes the sharp critter one look to get the message. If even this isn't enough to frighten a coyote off, it'll become suspicious and circle to pick up the caller's scent.

Calling coyotes at night might be challenging, but it isn't impossible. I've called literally thousands of them. I've even taken flash pictures of them, and if you know anything about photography, you know they have to be plenty close for that.

Another myth that Winston and I disproved early on was that you couldn't call a coyote to a light. The accepted practice was to

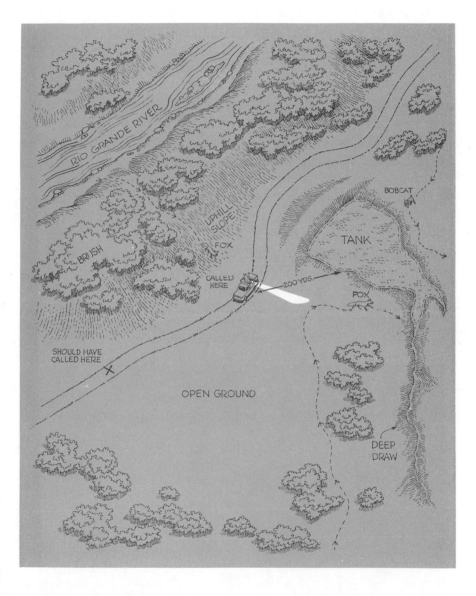

This shows what can happen if you don't know the lay of the land. The stock tank and deep draw were barriers the animals didn't want to cross. Moving a few hundred yards more down the pasture road would have been beneficial.

leave the light off as you called, periodically switch it on briefly to look, then cut it off again. But we had no problem calling coyotes to a light. One thing for sure, you'll see a lot more game if you switch your light on and leave it on. You can't see in the dark.

During our early learning years we used a conventional white headlight, but we were continually experimenting. One thing we tried was an overvoltage bulb like the PR-13 with a two-volt system. The light output was barely enough to see what we were doing, but it picked up eyes out about 50 yards out and animals showed no fear of the weak light. We figured this was because the light source was dim. Only much later did I fully understand the reason. With inadequate power, the overvoltage bulb burned red, creating a weak red beam, the forerunner of the red-lens light in widespread use today for calling varmints at night.

As far as I know, Winston and I developed the red-light system. It wasn't an original idea, that I'll admit. We'd heard that the Bronx Zoo in New York manipulated light to fool animals into thinking

The bobcat's eyes glow even in a weak light.

day was night and vice versa. Animals primarily prowl at night, but people visit the zoo during the day. So someone came up with an ingenious scheme for changing the animals' habits by using light. At night the cages were bathed in brilliant white light, simulating sunshine, whereas during the day the cages were darkened, illuminated only by a soft red light.

Studies of the animals' behavior indicated that they couldn't "see" the red light, or at least paid no attention to it. This conclusion made sense in that anything red comes out black when photographed with black-and-white film. Whether or not wild animals like the coyote can see colors is open to debate, but it's pretty much accepted that their ability to distinguish various colors isn't nearly as good as that of humans.

We were intrigued by this red-light theory. If it would fool animals in a zoo, why wouldn't it work in the wild? Our first model was simply a sheet of red cellophane rubber-banded over the lens of an ordinary headlight. From the beginning, the results we had with what I call the "no scare" light were phenomenal. It must have been a good idea because just about everybody has copied it.

Nowadays, we make lights with interchangeable covers that snap onto the lens. You can go from conventional white light to red merely by adding the red cover. One thing I learned later is that the red cover eliminates the heat, and this is a primary reason why a red beam is effective. A predator's eyes can't tolerate the heat of a white light.

Yet, even with a red light you can't ignore certain precautions. One thing you don't want to do is swing the light aimlessly about while walking toward your calling site. I adjust it so the headlight beam spills right in front of my feet. I never look up or glance around until I get where I'm going. Then I tilt the light so the beam shoots into the air. This way, when I raise my head, the beam won't flash against the brush or trees. I don't bring the light down until I'm ready to begin calling.

This procedure might seem too cautious, but I'm convinced that little things make the difference in successful calling. I've tested my light ideas on deer many times. If, for example, I walked through a field and swung the light around, any deer feeding nearby would

A gray fox will rush right in close at night.

get nervous and some of them would run. But with the beam down, I could walk furtively through the field and not scare any of the deer, even though some of them were so close I could hear them chewing. If you can fool a whitetail deer with a light, you can fool 'most any wild animal.

One problem with a red- or orange-lens headlight is that light output is reduced, so you have to keep the beam on the ground to pick up eyes as you sweep the light around. Some callers feel more comfortable with an ordinary white light, which will do the job if you pay attention to what you're doing. You have to tilt the beam upward so the ground is only faintly illuminated by the outer fringe of light as you call. This light is sufficient to detect eyes, yet an oncoming animal won't be spooked by the harsh beam. It also pays to have a hood on the light to see better, for one thing, and to eliminate the spill or splash of light that hits you and your companion and makes it easier to a predator to see your telltale shape.

If you call from a vehicle at night, you can use a bright red-lens spotlight that plugs into the cigarette lighter. I use a spotlight occasionally, but most times I wear only a headlight, which leaves

It is much easier to call 'coons at night than it is during the day.

both hands free and it is less tiring. After a few hours of holding a heavy spotlight and swinging it back and forth, your arm muscles will ache.

The easiest way to hunt is from a pickup bed. Before I go calling, I take everything out of the bed that might rattle or get in the way as the callers move about. I also spread a piece of old carpet to absorb noise. I believe wild animals are more afraid of banging noises than they are of motor vehicle noises. But of all noise, I guess talking is about the worst. The sound of the human voice puts terror into most wild animals.

Some callers build special platforms above pickup beds to get more elevation when calling. I have called from the top of a cab-over pickup camper. One of the most convenient adaptations is to put a camper shell on the bed and cut a couple of holes in the roof, large enough so a man can stand in the pickup with only his shoulders and head protruding through the roof. This not only keeps

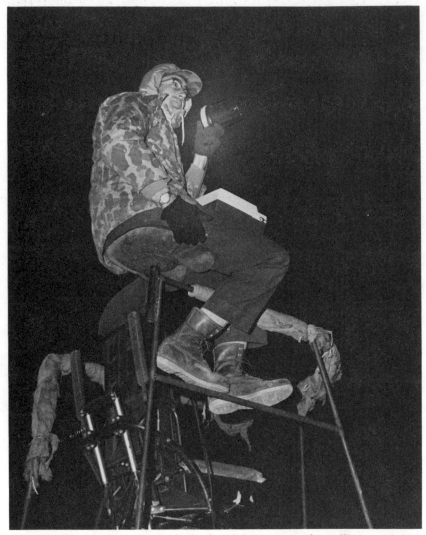

I built this platform in the bed of a pickup to use for calling at night.

the callers hidden, it keeps them out of the weather, and a cold north wind can be brutal in the winter. This arrangement gives you a place to rest your guns and lights, and you can lean on your elbows to take some of the strain off your feet. But most camper shells are either shiny aluminum or white, so you'll need to kill the reflection by spraying the shell with a dark-colored dull paint. A primer coat is good because it doesn't shine.

If possible, I like to hunt when there's no moon. Even the faint illumination of a partial moon makes it easier for a varmint to see you and more difficult for you to detect eyes. If you hunt on nights when the moon will be out, try to do your calling before the moon comes up or after it goes down.

For night calling, preparation and organization are vital. Scout the country during the daytime to pick and mark your calling sites. Things look entirely different at night, and you don't want to have to shine your light around to see what a site looks like.

J. D. Taylor and I hunt together regularly, and we believe in planning and teamwork. When we pick a place to call, we mark where we're going to stop the vehicle, to the exact foot. Just a few feet too many in either direction can change the whole scene.

I want as uncluttered a view as possible. When surveying a potential calling site, I pace back and forth, pausing periodically to look. I try to line up as many bushes and trees as possible, one right behind the other. Otherwise, you have bushes and trees scattered all over, obstructions a varmint can hide behind. Animals have the habit of passing behind a bush or tree just about the time you're ready to shoot. By lining up the obstructions, you reduce the number of hiding places and, at the same time, improve your odds by leaving more openings. That's why J. D. and I mark the exact spot; a few feet in either direction can make a whole lot of difference.

When we stop the vehicle, J. D. and I gingerly open and close the doors simultaneously. This reduces what little noise there is to half. We quietly climb into position without talking. Everything has been worked out in advance. In our scouting we've tried to predict the likely wind direction and that's the way we face, with all the bushes and trees lined up to reduce the clutter, as I explained.

We take turns calling. At one stop I call and J. D. does the shooting, and at the next stop we reverse roles. The person doing the calling also handles the headlight and shooting light. The shooter sits on a stool and waits until he receives a signal. He keeps out of the way by sitting below the rotating headlight of the caller, who's standing.

When the caller sees an animal's eyes approaching slowly, he nudges the shooter with his foot. But if the animal's hurrying, the

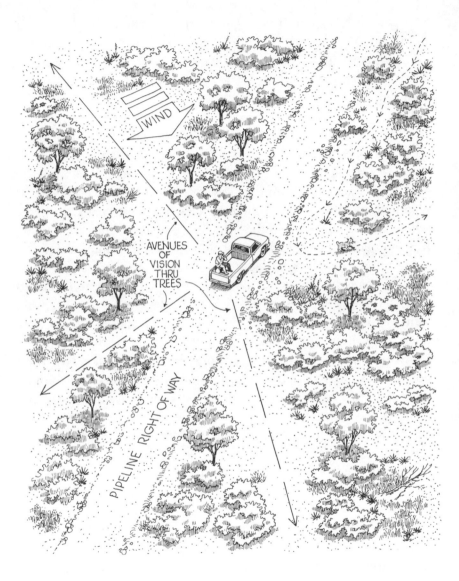

By scouting and marking your calling sites during the day, you can locate places where you have the best visibility.

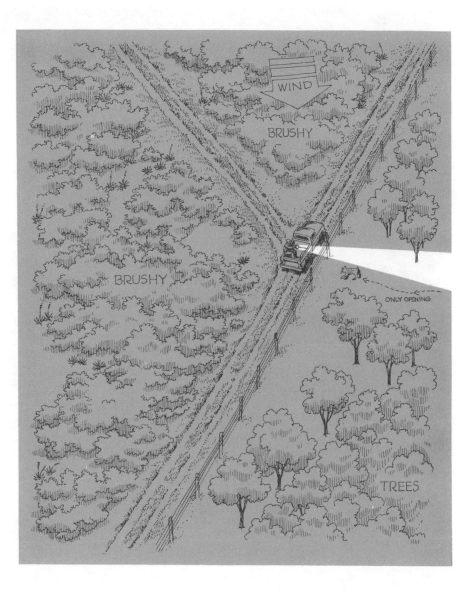

By utilizing the only opening through the trees and brush, I was able to see in that direction, plus along the pasture roads.

By keeping the light beam slightly in front of and above the animal's eyes, you won't scare it, and with a light-shy coyote, you can actually turn the critter your way.

caller kicks more forcefully. Like in baseball, the different signals eliminate confusion.

If I'm the shooter and J. D. signals, I immediately stand up and point the scoped rifle in the direction of his headlight beam. I know where the animal is because the beam will be held just above the eyes. When J. D. flashes on the shooting light, I'm looking right at the animal and I'm ready to shoot.

Yes, teamwork pays off. If you organize the hunt properly, fewer things can go wrong.

Chapter 11

Crows, Quail, Ducks, and Doves

The temptation was too great. Russell Tinsley, Winston, and I were bowhunting for deer along the Niobrara River near Bassett in northern Nebraska, but on this sunny, bright October afternoon, it was difficult to concentrate on the business at hand. Overhead, waves of crows passed beyond the treetops as they headed south. Some of the black birds dropped into the timber to rest.

That night we discussed the crows' migration. Winston already had an eight-point buck hanging outside the camp trailer. Russell and I had only a couple more days to hunt, but since we'd all brought shotguns, we decided to take advantage of the opportunity. We would hunt deer early and late and spend the rest of the day going after crows.

In midmorning we drove to another place we knew. We didn't want to shoot crows in the same area where we were hunting deer.

After parking the pickup and walking along to look for a place to call, we heard the familiar "caw, caw" of crows in the surrounding timber. When we found a likely spot, we put a plastic owl decoy and three fake crows where they easily could be seen. Then we hid and I began blowing on a crow call.

Soon a lone crow came wheeling overhead, swooping low. In

I like to use both owl and crow decoys.

camouflage and tucked back against bushes, we must have been concealed because the crow went at the decoys and ignored us. That was a mistake. As the crow crossed in front of us, both Russell and Winston fired and it tumbled head over end.

I continued to call. Only a minute or two after the sentinel had fallen, a flock of crows descended on us. With a screech, one sighted the owl decoy. Others started hollering excitedly. The birds were working themselves into a frenzy.

They made a couple of passes at the decoys, getting closer each time. They were no more than 20 yards away when I removed the call and said, "Now!" All three of us came up shooting. The action was brief, but when it was all over we had nine birds down.

Any kind of natural cover can be utilized when crow calling.

This was vintage crow hunting—fast and furious. The action might last only a few seconds, but that's long enough to drain an unplugged shotgun.

Perhaps crow hunting can be had near where you live. The bird is widespread. The most common is the Eastern crow, which migrates through the heart of the United States in the fall and spring. Other subspecies include the Southern, Western, and Florida crows. But basically, all four are the same: wily crafty birds that have survived and multiplied despite man's best control efforts.

The crow is hated because it is destruction masquerading as a bird. Crows usually travel in large flocks, and when they all invade a field to eat, it can cost a farmer in lost grain. That's why it isn't difficult to find places to hunt; most farmers welcome anyone who will help remove the pests.

You can choose from two methods of hunting crows: let them come to you, or go to them. If you know of a roost such as the one at Fort Cobb Reservoir in Oklahoma, you have it made. Thousands of birds often gather in one of these roosts. In early morning the crows scatter from the roost, heading in all directions to feed, and toward dusk they return along the same flight patterns. By observing these flyways you can determine where to situate yourself to intercept the flying birds.

For this hunting, I prefer an electronic caller. With an amplifier and speaker, the volume is sufficient to attract crows from long distances. The electronic caller leaves the hunter's hands free for shooting, and it's obviously easy on the lungs. The two tapes I prefer are crow distress cries or the shrieking, agitated voices of crows fighting an owl or hawk. Of the two, I think the crow distress cry is the best in most situations.

When calling, it's imperative you be well hidden and motionless. Crows are super wary. I use complete camouflage with a headnet, but I wear black gloves instead of camo colored. The dark gloves look like crows when I move my hands and, in fact, act as decoys. Anything overhead that obscures you but doesn't obstruct your field of view is a plus. I like to hunt from an old, abandoned farm building, shooting out a window or a door.

If it's up in the day and the flights have stopped, but the crows

One way to hide is to simply get beneath a piece of mesh camo cloth.

are in the field, one way to get some shooting is for three hunters to drive a vehicle into the field. The crows will retreat, but not far. They're curious and want to watch what's going on. Two hunters should get out of the vehicle near the edge of the field to find a place to hide. The other should drive away in the vehicle. After a short wait to let things settle down, calling can begin. One thing crows are incapable of is counting. When they see the vehicle leaving, they think the danger is gone.

If you've ever observed crows, you know they always post a sentinel or two when they're feeding in a field or meadow. If the sentinel sees anything suspicious it'll report to the others with that "caw, caw" alarm signal. And before the crows return to the field, the

An abandoned farm building makes a convenient hiding place when calling crows.

sentinel will check to be sure the danger is gone. If you're calling with an owl-fight sound or crow distress cries and a sentinel comes to survey the scene, it's important that you quit calling and remain motionless, in order to confuse the bird and keep it milling about— or, as a last resort, you can shoot the scout. Otherwise, the sentinel will hurry back and tell its companions that the whole thing is a hoax. If the sentinel fails to return to the flock immediately, the gang will soon appear to find out what's going on. The crows will come quick and low.

Even if you don't have access to a roost, crows may be residing in your area. These birds normally will be scattered, in smaller flocks. I like to hunt these crows by driving into a likely area, walking a couple hundred yards from the vehicle, putting an owl decoy and about three crow decoys where they can be seen, pushing back against any bush where the camouflage will blend into the surroundings, and going to work on a call. For this hunting, I simply use my crow call. I don't have to call very long in one place, and I have more mobility.

When crows show and you get a brief flurry of action, move on to another spot, driving maybe a quarter mile to call again. It isn't unusual to call crows most every time you stop.

Scouting for likely crow-hunting territory is pretty easy. You can look for the birds, but it's much easier to drive around and stop periodically to listen. Crows can't keep their big mouths shut, and a chorus of voices carries for a long, long way.

Hunting the magpie of the West isn't much different from crow hunting. It surprises me that more people don't hunt magpies. Magpies are sporty, and while they are not as sharp as crows, they're still not dumb bunnies. Look for them along the valleys in the farmlands. They, like crows, raid grainfields. Hide along a brushy fence row or even in a barn. Magpies really come to my short-range predator call.

One trick is to collect dead magpies and put them beside you. When others are attracted to the call, wait for them to get close and then toss the dead magpies at them. This really drives the others crazy and they will start screeching, attracting other magpies. You can wait until you have a bunch milling around before you commence shooting.

It's important to down the sentinel before it can alert the others.

While you bring crows and magpies to you, a quail call can be used to locate coveys. You suck on the quail call to make the familiar bobwhite sound. It's easy and effective.

I use the quail call to locate coveys when I'm hunting with a dog. This way you can spend more time effectively hunting than simply wandering around at random, hoping the dog picks up the scent. You can also get into more open country toward dusk and use the

The dove call—with its familiar "coo-coo" sound—is primarily a locator call.

call to locate roosting coveys to hunt first thing the next morning. This way you can also get a fairly good idea of the number of coveys in the area you're hunting.

The quail call also is effective for locating single quail when a covey is busted. The single quail will be upset when it's away from the bunch, so when you suck on the call you'll usually get a prompt reply.

A dove call also is a locator call. About the only thing to be said for it is when you make the "coo, coo" sound, a mourning dove likely will answer. If you're jump shooting doves in timber, you can pretty much determine in which trees the birds are taking their midday rest.

Ducks and geese, of course, are attracted to calls. Don't be fooled into thinking that calling waterfowl is all that difficult. If you master

I called and shot this duck on a pond on my ranch in central Texas.

a feed call to draw attention to your decoys, I don't think you'll need much else.

But my experience with waterfowl is limited. Unfortunately, the waterfowl seasons come when it's legal to hunt deer and then call predators during the fur season. I don't have enough time to do everything I want to do. I've got to have priorities.

I hunt ducks two, maybe three times a season, mostly on the ranch ponds near my home. We have many large reservoirs not far away where the ducks spend the night, but come morning they begin arriving at the ponds to feed.

I scout the ponds the previous afternoon to determine which ones are the most popular with the ducks. I return before daybreak, pitch out a few decoys, and hide. When I see ducks approaching, I beckon to them with the feed call. Unless they see something suspicious, they plunge in close, circling to head into the wind as they drop toward the decoys.

If several of us are hunting together, we'll be in position on scattered ponds by legal shooting time. Thus, if ducks show at the pond where I'm hunting and I get a shot or two, the birds likely will fly to another nearby pond and try to land again—and blunder into another ambush.

Chapter 12

Outfox a Squirrel

Anybody who's a proficient squirrel hunter will be skilled at hunting anything. This little critter is a good teacher. Don't be misled by the behavior of city-park squirrels; they're like zoo animals that become accustomed to and comfortable with humans. A wild squirrel is something else. It's a bundle of nerves and is as alert as anything in the woods.

But besides being a teacher, a squirrel is fun to hunt. I remember what Ted Clark said after we'd been hunting squirrels one clear October morning. With the temperature warming, it was urgent we get the squirrels skinned and on ice. Clark had removed his camouflage top and was on one knee, washing a carcass in the small spring-fed stream. He paused briefly, turned his head, and said, "You know, this has been fun. I enjoy squirrel hunting as much as I do deer hunting."

Now, to anyone who has hunted squirrels, this might not be much of a revelation. But Clark is director of wildlife for the Texas Parks and Wildlife Department. To equate the squirrel with the whitetail in the deer-obsessed state where I live is flirting with heresy, but it tells you something about the man and the sport. Clark told me that when he was growing up in Alvin, a town not far from Houston, his first hunting was for squirrels. While he's since hunted every other type of animal found in the state, his love for squirrel hunting has never diminished.

With a couple of squirrels in the bag, I'm looking for another to answer.

"I don't care how much you know, squirrels can still teach you something about hunting," he said.

That's for sure.

The ubiquitous squirrel is second only to the cottontail rabbit as our most popular game animal. It's readily available in most locales, and hunting seasons generally are liberal. The most widespread species is the gray (cat) squirrel, which prefers heavy woods. The larger fox squirrel likes a more open environment with scattered timber. Most of my experience has been with fox squirrels because they're the only kind of tree squirrel found in central Texas, where I live.

But the squirrel hunting I've had in other parts of Texas and in other states has convinced me of one thing: a squirrel is a squirrel, no matter where you find it. Don't be fooled by its size. You have to know what you're doing if you want to eat squirrel with any regularity.

To do this, the first order of business is to be in the woods at the first hint of dawn. Squirrels are most active from daylight until an hour or two after sunrise.

There's more to it, of course, than merely going into the woods. You have to know where to go. Scouting is as important in squirrel hunting as in other types of hunting. You need to come up with a game plan. First off, you determine what the squirrels are eating; that puts you in their range. Then you study the lay of the land to figure the best approach and the best place to hide for effective hunting. This is an orderly process similar to a detective gathering evidence.

In autumn, when most squirrel seasons open, the bushytails are feeding primarily on mast—nuts like acorns, pecans, hickory nuts, beechnuts, and butternuts. In my country the number one food is the pecan; squirrels love this succulent nut.

Before a squirrel eats a nut, it shucks off the shell—and there's your clue. Search for these "cuttings" beneath hardwood trees. In the sprawl of a hardwood grove, squirrels likely will be scattered. Nuts don't ripen uniformly; a few trees always mature quicker than the others. And it's not uncommon to find several squirrels working just one or two trees.

Let's return for a moment to that hunt with Ted Clark. I must admit I took advantage. When Clark, Russell Tinsley, and Leroy Gebert showed up before daybreak, I scattered them in the pecan bottom along a creek and left them to do the best they could. I walked to some trees a few hundred yards away where I'd located squirrels the previous morning. I'd done this with both my eyes

The fox squirrel is one of the easiest of all animals to call.

and my ears. I'd found considerable cuttings, but only after sitting for more than a half hour and simply listening. Squirrels are vocal and by listening for them, I was able to pinpoint the general area where they were feeding.

When I got settled, it was still gloomy dark under the thick-leafed trees, but I could hear a squirrel already rustling about some-where above me. I took my Burnham Bros. Squirrel Call from my shirt pocket and tapped on it. The first series of soft barks is all it took; the squirrel came around the tree trunk not 10 feet away and I shot it in the head.

Without moving, I eventually put five squirrels on the ground. Clark, Tinsley, and Gebert together got a total of one. That should tell you something about the importance of scouting.

By going into the woods to look and listen, you might be surprised to find squirrels where you didn't expect them to be. Other than nuts, they could be feeding on corn or wild fruit or even something else.

On a creek behind my house there's a fig tree. For several mornings I'd hear squirrel chatter from that direction. Curiosity finally got to me. Just at first light I put on my camouflage clothing, grabbed my .22 rifle, and eased that way. When I returned to the house less than an hour later, I had four plump squirrels cleaned and skinned. They'd been feeding on ripe figs. (This was in late summer; there's no closed season on squirrels in the western two-thirds of Texas.)

One of the first things you learn about squirrels is you can't be haphazard and careless if you want to outfox them. You have to stay hidden—I wear complete camouflage, even a headnet—and you have to remain motionless. The squirrel has fantastic eyesight and hearing.

You can merely look and find squirrels, but I enjoy calling them into the open. A fox squirrel is one of the easiest of all wild animals to dupe with a call (but all squirrels communicate by barking, most commonly to alert others to the presence of danger, and even the run-happy gray squirrel is gullible).

The type of call I use is easily operated by tapping on the thin-rubber ball, which pushes air through a perforated diaphragm to imitate squirrel barking. You cup one hand around the metal housing holding the diaphragm and push the sound into this hand to get the proper throaty tone. Without the muffle, the sound would be too high pitched.

The call I prefer is rapid-fire barking, the sound an angry squirrel makes. Tap the call to create three or four sharp, distinct barks, followed by a rapid outburst, produced by tapping the call as fast as you can. The call doesn't have to be loud; in the early morning

To give the call its throaty tone, cup your hand around the end to regulate the sound.

calm, a squirrel can hear the barking for a long distance. But don't call continuously. Call briefly, then shut up and give the squirrels' curiosity time to work.

Sometimes a squirrel might come to within 50 or so yards of you, only to stop and look. Its tail will tell you something about its state of mind. If it's barking and pumping its tail up and down, you've got it worked up and it's ready for more. If you call again, don't be surprised to see the squirrel come running toward you.

There are times, however, when a squirrel won't answer a call, particularly in the morning when the animals are done with their daily activities. They're taking things easy and don't want any trouble, so they'll ignore you.

When this happens, I leave the woods and head home. If I stay with it, I might get another squirrel or two, but the effort isn't worth it. I hunt at the squirrels' convenience—when they're active—not at my convenience.

When calling squirrels, I like to use a .22 rifle. It is more sporty, for one thing, and, in the loose timber where fox squirrels are found, shots likely will be beyond the range of a shotgun. I suppose I was the first hunter in my part of the country to put a big-game scope on a .22 rifle, an idea that has been much copied. The larger one-inch scope is much sharper and far superior to the small-diameter .22 scope for gathering and intensifying light. With a bigger scope sight, you can get a clear picture long before you even see open sights.

But if you're in thick woods and you're after the gray squirrel—which will take off running at the slightest excuse—you might be better off with a shotgun. Also, some landowners welcome only shotgun hunters; they're leery of the long-shooting rifles.

One advantage of the rifle is you'll be pressed into situations where you must do some quick snap shooting. This is invaluable training for any type of hunting. Learning to shoot proficiently is only a matter of practice, and I can't think of any better practice than on squirrels.

Getting one in your riflesight is the main priority. Calling is just one of the tricks. I've learned others through the years.

Picture this situation. You're hidden and motionless when you see a fox squirrel in an isolated tree about 100 yards away. The bushytail is busy feeding and ignores your call. Slipping in closer is impossible, considering the open country and the wariness of your quarry.

If the squirrel isn't suspicious and doesn't know you're there, try rushing the tree. Get there as rapidly as you can, surprising the

I prefer to hunt squirrels with a .22 rifle; it's good practice.

bushytail before it can flee. Often it'll freeze tight and you can get a quick shot.

Even if it does run, it likely will dash into the leafy treetop to hide. Stand still a few minutes and watch. Curiosity may eventually make the squirrel take a peek to see what's going on. Or a soft tapping of your call might draw it into the open.

But periodically you'll meet up with a sharp squirrel that seemingly vanishes into thin air. What happens is, when you move, the squirrel moves. As you circle the tree to look, the squirrel sidles around the tree trunk or branch, keeping out of sight.

You can short-circuit this trickery by picking up a fallen limb and tossing it to the opposite side of the tree. The squirrel will be startled by the sudden noise and scramble around the tree trunk—right into your gunsight.

If you're hunting with a buddy, stand motionless and let him slowly circle the tree. The squirrel will try to hide from him and will slide around to where you'll have a clear shot.

But if the squirrel simply sprawls atop a limb, way up high, there isn't much you can do except look, studying each limb, trying to pick out the squirrel. If the squirrel gets careless it might allow its bushy tail to droop off one side of the limb and you'll be able to see it moving back and forth with the breeze.

One of these now-you-see-me, now-you-don't squirrels forces you to concentrate and search intently, training your eyes to pick the animal out of its natural surroundings. Learning to "see" game is a major step toward successful hunting.

Chapter 13

Talkin' Turkey

To call someone a turkey is to imply he's sort of stupid. But don't call a wild turkey a turkey; it's one smart hombre.

A wild turkey gobbler isn't difficult to call, however, if you pay attention to what you're doing. During the spring mating season, the tom is juiced up and looking for any willing female. If your call convinces him you're a lovesick hen seeking companionship, he'll come courting. But at the same time he'll be quick to notice anything unusual or out of the ordinary. Calling a gobbler is one thing; shooting him is something else. During that critical time when a turkey appears and the scene comes into sharp focus, many things can go wrong and something usually does.

I've called a few turkeys in the fall, when a flock was scattered and the birds were trying to get back together; but spring hunting is much more dependable and exciting. There's nothing quite like the sight of a proud gobbler strutting about, his wattles brilliant red, his wing tips making sort of a booming sound as he drags them along the ground. I've called many turkeys just to watch them or to take pictures. One time before the spring season, I went on a photo session near Rocksprings in midwestern Texas, to a ranch where there were many turkeys. Five gobblers came to my call simultaneously. They were in a straight line like a marching military formation. That was something.

Notice the marks on either side of the footprints where the strutting gobbler dragged his wing tips on the ground.

Five at once was very unusual, of course. Most times I feel fortunate to call one. Gobblers don't always cooperate. Don't be misled into believing you're home free simply because you've succeeded in getting a turkey to gobble in answer to your call. A tom might answer, but if he's in the company of one or more hens, he isn't going to leave them.

Calling a turkey is a matter of timing, location, and position, among other factors. I'd guess location is the most important consideration, because if no turkey's available to be called, you aren't going to call one. It's that simple.

I scout not only during the season, but beforehand as well. I move around in known turkey country early or late in the day and listen. If a gobbler's undisturbed, it won't take much to make him reveal his position. Sometimes the slamming of a vehicle door will make one gobble. I use an owl, crow, or predator call. Blow on one of these and the gobbler normally will answer.

You'll want to pinpoint the area where turkeys are roosting. A few turkeys will stay at the old roost, but others will scatter. The gobblers generally go where the hens go, but an old, solitary gobbler might move around a lot. He'll roost in one place for several nights, then move on to roost in another place. I've located many gobblers then lost them before I had a chance to hunt.

If possible, I like to "put a gobbler to roost," as the saying goes—locating him one evening, then returning the next morning to try to call him.

Before you do this, you'll have to master the basics of calling. Most beginners make calling more complicated than it really is. Of all the fundamentals of turkey calling, the importance of the actual sound or call probably is the most overrated. The "yelp" of a hen is the only call you need under most circumstances.

I'd suggest learning on a box-type call or some other call you manipulate by hand. Later you might want to try a mouth-type call.

Forget about those other sounds such as clucking, cackling, and the kee-kee run. Practice until you have confidence in the yelping sound. The idea is to call a turkey, not to see how many sounds you can play on a call. Calling a turkey or two will build your confidence. Then you can start thinking about more sophisticated tricks.

But first things first. You've located a gobbler's roost during your scouting. Return to the woods before daylight and slip to within about 150 yards of the roost. Don't make the mistake of getting too close; you might make the turkey suspicious or actually spook him. This usually isn't the case, however. The gobble of a turkey is deceptive in the early morning calm, and you're usually not as close to his roost as you think you are. For this reason, give him plenty of time to show. Many callers get impatient and leave before their quarry makes an appearance.

Once you're hidden near the roost, you've taken care of the first factor: location. If the turkey is gobbling, you can assume the second factor—timing—is covered as well. That leaves position.

You don't want to hide where you're watching wide-open country. Gobblers like to follow a line of brush, staying out of sight. I've called them across clearings, but there was brush all around. Instinctive caution tells the tom to have an escape route nearby should danger arise.

And gobblers simply refuse to come in certain directions. You can be calling in one place and getting a regular answer, but not

A gobbler with a beard like this is a real prize.

be able to fool the turkey. Yet, if you change your position, the old bird comes a-running.

Why this is, I don't know. Bruce Brady and I have discussed it numerous times. Bruce lives in Brookhaven, Mississippi, and he's a superskilled turkey caller of long experience. He thinks some places are like sacred ground; the gobbler refuses to cross that area, no matter what. I believe this is because the direction is not a path the turkey normally follows. Turkeys have certain trails and routes they prefer and just won't travel in other directions. When a gobbler refuses to come, you may as well change position. Otherwise, you'll be wasting your time.

When I change positions, I make a quarter circle around the bird's position, going 200 or maybe even 300 yards before I hide and try calling again. Even after going this far, I'm still only about 150 yards from where I think the gobbler is. But when you move like this, you must be furtive and cautious. If the gobbler hears or sees you, or even senses your presence, that's it.

As you make this quartering circle, you need to know the lay of the land. Otherwise, you might wander far from the gobbler when you think you're still close to him. The more you've scouted, the better prepared you'll be.

While a gobbler refuses to follow some directions, he might not be able to follow others. I remember such a place on a ranch I was hunting for the first time. This gobbler was really carrying on. From all indications, he was excited and everything was going according to plan. I was calling and he was answering but, strangely, nothing was happening.

Something was wrong. After more than a quarter hour of steady exchange, I decided to slip that way and steal a peek, hoping I could get close to the gobbler without alarming him. When I did get a glimpse, it became obvious why he hadn't approached my position. He was in a neighbor's pasture, running back and forth along the hog-wire fence, stopping to strut and drag his wings and gobble every time I stroked the call. The turkey is a wary and crafty bird, but some of its mannerisms border on stupidity. This was a low fence and the gobbler easily could have flown over it, but instead he just ran back and forth in confusion. I've seen turkeys fight a fence for so long they actually make deep trails where they have run.

If you have a tom answering, call in rhythm with his gobbles. All turkeys have different rhythms. And if you happen to hit a sour note, immediately come back with the correct sound. If a gob-

If I'm not sitting in a bush, I like to get in front of it rather than behind; I can see better this way.

bler's interested, he isn't going to pay that much attention to a bad call.

And be patient. If you think you've located a gobbler, give him at least 15 minutes to show. Even if he isn't answering, tempt him with a series of yelps every minute or so. A tom might be coming, but not telling you he is. I've called gobblers that suddenly showed up when I'd no idea they were even interested.

I remember one gobbler in particular. I'd been hearing this tom near my home for several days before I got the chance to hunt him. I set up a place and called for maybe five minutes, then moved and tried again. The gobbler never answered.

On my fifth try, right at sundown, I hid along a cleared highline right-of-way. When I stroked the call the first time I saw the gobbler coming from a long way off. The distance was so far he appeared to be only a moving speck. He came on the dead run, hesitating only when I hit the call. Then he would stop long enough to strut, drag his wings, and gobble before running again. By the time he was within shooting range, he was panting from exhaustion.

This tom came from the very direction where I'd been calling earlier. It wasn't hard to figure out what happened. All the time I was moving about and calling, he wanted to come, but I wasn't giving him time. Finally, I had him worked up to the point of being almost crazy. He ran down the cleared right-of-way, forgetting all nature's rules of survival.

Unlike other callers I've hunted with, I prefer to stand rather than sit when calling, if conditions permit. This gives me more flexibility. Dad always preached the importance of being ready. If a turkey shows, I'm ready. I look for a bush that's a little taller than head high. Ideally, it will branch out about shoulder height. I wiggle into the bush and rest my gun over a limb, pointing in the direction from which I expect a turkey to come. I wear a camo headnet and obscure my head with a few loose limbs and so nothing suggests I'm there. With the gun already in position, little motion is lost when I decide to shoot.

If you must move, make it a controlled movement. If you need to shift positions, watch the turkey's head and don't do anything until it's behind a bush or tree. I move only when I'm ready to shoot. I select the position that I think will give me the best shot. The bird will immediately notice my slight movement and plough to a halt. I aim at the head because the mass of wing feathers won't permit adequate penetration. Many arguments have been waged over the merits of No. 4 versus No. 6 shot. The size of the shot isn't that important. What's important is how your shotgun patterns shot of any size. Some guns will pattern No. 4 better than 6, or vice versa. I believe in patterning a shotgun and knowing exactly what it does. I want the shot size that gives the best or tightest pattern out to about 40 yards. Also, before I start to call, I like to step off the distance to any landmarks like rocks, stumps, or bushes. This way I know my exact range. In the excitement that ensues when a gobbler shows, distance can be deceptive. The tom may look farther off than he really is, and you'll miss your shot.

But if you make a mistake before you're ready and the turkey sees your movement, you can wave goodbye as he leaves. A turkey

When calling, I like to rest my gun across a bush or limb. This way I can shoot with minimal motion.

can appear and disappear quicker than any creature I know. If the tom gives a startled "putt," he's leaving. He puts his feathers down—what I call "trimming his running gear." With their long-legged gait, turkeys can really move.

I once read that tests revealed a turkey's eyes have about 10 times the resolving power of a human's. Its angle of vision is 270° and it's not color blind. With my country-boy thinking, I have a problem in comprehending such things, but I don't need scientists to tell me about turkeys. I've seen and respect their abilities.

One fall I was bowhunting, sitting in a carefully prepared blind in a leafy live oak. Around the platform, nailed in a fork, was a wire from which I'd hung green cedar limbs. Only my head was showing, and it was covered by a camo headnet. Even my shiny bow was camouflaged.

Sitting motionless, I saw a half-dozen wild turkeys coming down the trail. When the birds approached to within about 40 yards, they unexpectedly stopped and stared at me a few seconds. Then one gave a startled "putt" and they took off. Hidden as I was, not moving a muscle, that performance made a lasting impression on me. They knew something about the whole deal was unnatural and they didn't stick around to find out what it was.

One advantage of calling turkeys is they can't smell, although they compensate for this deficiency with their fantastic eyesight and hearing. Turkeys are just naturally suspicious. Don't try calling in a strong or gusty wind. Turkeys, like any wild creatures, don't like the wind because the noise created by the movement of branches makes it more difficult to detect danger. In addition, gobblers can't hear calls in the wind.

While all this sounds complicated, it isn't. With everything that's been written about turkey hunting, I can understand how a beginner might be confused. Most of the advice is contradictory. One "expert" recommends calling steadily, while another says to call sparingly. What this tells me is that there's no "best" way to call turkeys. You have to work out your own style as you go along.

To be sure, much misinformation has been passed along about wild turkeys. It's been said that only a few gobblers breed the hens. An old tom is a male chauvinist; he stakes out his territory and collects a harem of hens, then posts a sign for other gobblers. Most

A wrong move right here and you can wave goodbye to this gobbler.

of the time this is true—but not always. If the spring hatch has been exceptional and many young gobblers are running together, they find strength in numbers, like a street gang, and will overwhelm an old gobbler. I've seen this happen several times. They want to pick a fight, but the old bird doesn't want to take them on. Their superior numbers tell him he doesn't stand a chance.

Under normal circumstances, wild turkeys have a pecking order that's settled real quick. I've learned this from raising a lot of wild turkeys on my ranch for observation and study, to learn all I can about their behavior.

Of my last three turkeys, one quickly whipped another then turned on the third. I missed the turkeys after nightfall; they weren't in their normal roost. With a flashlight, I walked into an adjacent field and found them still going at it. They had fought all day and on into the night. Their heads were bloody and they were completely exhausted. But they were determined to find which was the strongest, which was king. When this is eventually determined, Number 1 gets the first choice of everything—feed and hens—and the others won't challenge him.

This is important to know because sometimes a gobbler will come to your call quietly and tentatively. He wants to be with a hen, but at the same time he's afraid of the king gobbler. The inferior tom knows his role.

Such behavior confused Jim Zumbo. Jim had flown from his home in Utah to hunt with me. I had located some gobblers and we hid in the woods before first light. Down from us, along a pecan grove in a creek bottom, a gobbler already was sounding off. From the deep tone of his voice, I knew he must be big.

When the light was strong enough so we could tell shapes from shadows, I stroked the call. In no time flat, a turkey came walking toward us. He came tentatively, acting halfway scared. He was walking—not strutting—and watching cautiously. As gobblers go, he wasn't large—his beard was about two inches long. He was a juvenile gobbler, or a jake as the young male is sometimes called. But I expected Jim to shoot. When you don't have long to hunt, any gobbler is a shootable gobbler.

But Jim let the turkey walk on by and disappear into the brush. Later I asked him what had happened. He said the bird didn't act like a gobbler. He wanted to shoot, but he wasn't sure whether the bird was a gobbler or hen. He had just enough indecision to let the turkey escape.

It was just as well, as things worked out. Later that day, Jim shot a trophy—a tom with a beard more than 10 inches long. The moral of this story, I suppose, is that sometimes it pays to be unlucky.

Chapter 14

Elk are Exceptional

Maybe it's a combination of things—the immense size of the animal, the volume of its voice, the high country where sound carries for a long distance—but when it comes to the vigor of answering a call, nothing compares with the bull elk. He's in a class by himself. When he throws out his broad chest and lets go, the sound reverberates off the mountainsides, with each echo seemingly getting louder.

The elk's sound is called a bugle, but it might better be described as a whistle, starting low and gaining in pitch, through about five octaves. Various sound effects may accompany the bugle. A bull elk sort of reminds me of a Brahma bull, a huge, flop-eared species of cattle found in the arid Southwest. Both animals possess voices that almost shake trees. An old bull elk will grunt, bellow, groan, and squeal. After he whistles, he tapers off to a series of deep-throated grunts. You can get a pretty good idea of a bull elk's size by the sound of his voice. A young bull will do more high-pitched screeching.

Calling a bull elk is a thrill not to be forgotten. You can have this experience if you're in the right place at the right time. The place is the elk's summer range. The time is September, or maybe a few days into October. This is when elk are rutting. The peak of the rut normally comes with the full moon in September, especially if the full moon occurs around the middle of the month.

There's no thrill quite like that of a bull charging toward your call.

In most Western states, bugling has almost ceased by the time rifle season rolls around. At best, it's an on-and-off proposition. But during the early archery seasons it isn't unusual to hear a symphony of elk whistling—several bulls challenging one another—almost daily. This is especially true in areas where elk are abundant, and these big animals seem to be increasing and expanding their range all the time. I've known quite a few bowhunters who bugled elk close enough to get them with arrows. My friend Gary Calhoun, a Colorado outfitter, has called many elk for his clients, and some of the bulls have been real trophies.

You can learn the correct sound at home. A tape of a real bull will let you hear the actual whistle. An instruction record or tape is helpful to learn how to blow the call. The exact sounds are difficult to describe; you need to hear them. A hunter would be foolish not to take advantage of all the instructional material available today. I wish I'd had these aids back when I started. I had to learn the hard way—by trial and error.

When blowing the call, you don't need to burst your lungs. It's important to pace yourself so you have enough air to go through all the notes, low to high. And remember—in the high country the air is thin, so even more effort will be required. Learn to blow with an easy style that will give adequate volume. Don't worry that a bull will have trouble hearing you. At high altitude where the animals range in September, the sound can be heard for an incredibly long distance if you call from a ridge.

I like to get into my hunting territory a day or two before the season opens. This serves a twofold purpose: it lets me become

I go to work on a Burnham Bros. Elk Call in the Colorado high country.

acclimated to the altitude, and I also have time for scouting. I like to look around even if I'm familiar with the country. The elk might not be where they were last season. Once the season opens, you want to get into their range.

But simply getting acclimated isn't enough. When you go hunting in a state like New Mexico, Colorado, Idaho, or Wyoming, you want to be in top physical condition. You should start walking or jogging at least a month before your trip. Navigating through the high country takes a lot of extra stamina and energy.

When scouting, I like to be unobtrusive. I don't want to alarm the elk or even make them suspicious before the season opens. I've driven by elk hunters' camps in the high country and seen men and boys racing back and forth along logging roads on noisy trail bikes. Elks aren't foolish. The popping noise of a trail bike is unnatural and tells the elk to be wary. If I drive to my elk camp, I don't even start the pickup again—unless absolutely necessary—until I leave. You can't be too cautious.

If you're hunting during the rut, you might not have to do extensive scouting; the whistling bulls will let you know where they are. I've stood in one place and heard four bulls carrying on at the same time. Every time one would bugle, one or two more would answer in defiance. The bulls seem to be most vocal in the calm right before or after a storm. They also dislike warm weather; if the day becomes shirt-sleeves warm, the bulls will shut up.

The only sound I want a bull to hear is my call. That's why I like a quiet camp. During those more than two decades when Winston and I traveled to Colorado at least once each fall, we hunted where both elk and mule deer roamed. We'd hide our camp back in some timber and wouldn't chop wood, play a radio, or even build a campfire. We were super quiet. And almost every year we had elk come strolling right through our camp.

There are darn few quiet camps, however. We've been camped in the same area as other hunters and have been able to hear them talking several hundred yards away. Most people can't believe how far sound can carry in this country. Camping in thick timber will help muffle the noise, but most camps are pitched in the open.

By having a quiet camp, I can start hunting almost immediately after I leave. You've probably read stories of hunters who rode horses for miles before daybreak so they'd be in position to hunt when there was enough light to see. This traveling is necessary only because of camp noise.

If a bull whistles, I answer him. How he'll react, I can't predict. Every elk is different. One might come storming toward you, and you can hear him crashing through the timber long before he comes within sight. Or you might get a sneaky cuss that takes his own good time. Some elk won't come at all, one reason being that the bull won't budge from his territory.

I remember a conversation I once had with a big bull in the Uncompahgre National Forest of western Colorado. When he first whistled, I could tell he was some distance off. But once I started bugling with my call, his voice got stronger and I knew he was coming my way. He only came part way toward me before stopping, yet he continued to answer my call in a most excited manner.

We argued back and forth for quite some time. I knew something was wrong, but I didn't know what. Gingerly I sneaked in his direction so I could see off the high ground where I was calling. A bluff I hadn't known about stood between the bull and me. The bull refused to circle the bluff, so he just stood below and hollered

I shot this bull in the Uncompahgre National Forest in western Colorado.

his head off. I tried to ease around and get close enough for a shot, but the bull got away.

If you have a bull that won't leave his territory, try changing direction just as you do with an ornery turkey gobbler. The route between you and the prey might not be one he likes to travel. An elk is a brute of an animal. An average mature bull stands about five feet at the withers and weighs 600 to 700 pounds, although some exceptional bulls will go 1,000 pounds on the hoof, maybe a few pounds more. Yet despite this bulk, an elk can be hard to see. A crafty bull has a knack for staying hidden. Even when one is coming to a call, he likes to stay in the timber. If you move a few hundred yards, the direction change may give the bull a route he won't hesitate taking.

If a position change doesn't work, keep bugling but slam a heavy stick against brush, trees, and the ground between calls. This noise is meant to sound like two bulls fighting one another or one bull fighting the brush. This tactic gets the old rogue excited. He might be watching a harem of cows, but if he thinks an intruder is in or near his territory, he'll lose his cool and rush to run the other off.

A bull can work himself into a lather. I've watched a big bull gather cows in a tight bunch and try to watch them while keeping alert for other bulls. It isn't unusual for one or more smaller, inferior bulls to be lingering nearby, waiting for something to happen. If the big bull takes after a bull that strays too close, another bystander might run in and top a cow while the big bull's preoccupied.

I've had the opportunity just to watch a bunch of elk. Funny, but when Winston and I started going to Colorado, we were after trophy mule deer and simply ignored the elk, though back then both were legal during the same season and we easily could have purchased an elk license along with our deer license to go after both. But we didn't want to bother hunting elk.

I saw some bulls much bigger than anything I've killed. A couple might have made the record book. On several occasions, elk grazed all around me while I waited to ambush a deer.

But, in a way, our deer-only attitude was a blessing. You can learn much more about wildlife by observing than by shooting. In many instances the animal's behavior is contrary to what you might have read or heard.

An elk has a huge track, comparable to that of a young steer.

It didn't take me long to realize that an elk has a super nose. Let one get downwind from you and get a sniff of human scent and that's that. That's why, if I'm hunting with a buddy, I like one of us to call while the other hides about 100 yards downwind. The actual distance depends primarily on visibility. The two hunters should be in sight of each other, for safety's sake. Also, I like to communicate with hand signals. If I'm calling and see a bull coming but angling downwind, I can alert my buddy so he'll be ready to shoot when the animal steps into sight.

Don't depend on hearing an approaching elk before you see him. How such an immense animal can move through thick timber with almost ghostlike precision baffles me. But I've seen elk step out of the timber, real close, when I never had an inkling they were near.

If you have a recalcitrant bull that's answering you but won't come to your call, you can keep bugling while your buddy sneaks in his direction and hopes for a shot. You've got to watch those wind currents, though. They can be tricky in the mountains. And the stalk has to be slow and quiet. Elk have good hearing and eyesight. Their eyes may even be better than those of deer.

Bulls aren't likely to be in the open, so you'll have to go into the timber, which makes spotting an elk at a distance difficult, in spite of its jumbo size. Elk will be in or near cover generally, unless they're grazing in meadows and little parks early and late in the day.

More often than not, you'll be hunting when the bulls are mute, after the rut. You'll have to resort to hunting techniques other than calling.

Much elk hunting is done on horseback. I believe a horse walking through the woods is less likely to alarm an elk than a man is. But even on horseback it's important to be in your hunting territory by daylight, so you're ready to hunt the moment light is sufficient. Also avoid the temptation to ride around seeing the countryside. You're elk hunting not joy riding, and the only way you're going to find an elk is by looking and looking hard.

Every time you sight new country, dismount and use your binoculars to look it over. Depending on your field of view, this might take a half hour or longer. Don't leave until you're convinced you've

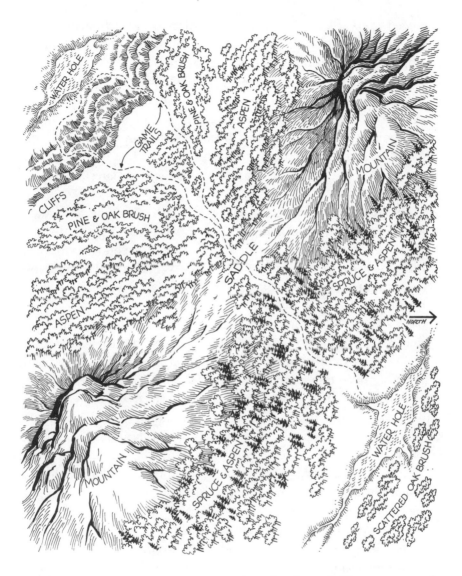

A saddle—a low place between mountains—is where elk like to cross, and it's a good place to wait in ambush.

glassed every foot of the country. Especially search shady areas, trees with low-hanging branches, and the slopes where elk like to bed, particularly if there's thick, dark spruce or what is called black timber. Elk like to bed facing downhill, usually with the wind at their backs so they can see or smell approaching danger. This vantage also provides access to a convenient escape route.

Although most hunters and outfitters like to move around to hunt, I've always been more of an ambush hunter. I like to locate a trail with fresh sign, get on it, and watch. Sooner or later an elk will come by.

The ideal trail connects a waterhole with a feeding area and a bedding area—and normally the three won't be a great distance apart. Few hunters go after elk this way, and I wonder why. One thing I learned during those years when Winston and I were after deer is that elk also travel trails regularly, and you can ambush them just as you can deer.

Elk like to bed along the benches on the north slopes in black timber, which lets in very little sunlight. Even in the coldest weather, I've consistently found elk bedded on the snow side or shade side of a hill or mountain. But the elk might cross to the other side of the mountain to feed and water. If so, the trail will be at a narrow place, a saddle, between connecting mountains, the easiest place to cross over. Find such a saddle with a trail that indicates heavy travel and you've got the perfect place to situate your stand.

Be on the trail at daylight, dressed comfortably in lots of clothes. You can always take something off, but you can't add clothing you haven't brought. If the sun passes behind a cloud, the air above 8,000 feet can become quite chilly. Stick it out as long as you can. If your feet get cold, get up and walk around until the blood is circulating again, then sit back down. I like to carry a piece of plastic to sit on. If your rump gets damp, you'll never get warm.

If I'm hunting with a group and we find a trail that's been traveled regularly, we take turns watching it. The trail never goes unattended. And surprisingly, some of the bigger bulls have been killed at the height of the day. A bull elk isn't going to bed down and stay in one place all day. He's going to get up and move, even for a short distance. As long as he's in the thick timber, he feels secure.

And even if elk don't move on their own, other hunters keep them stirring about.

A common mistake is to quit too early. Many hunters fear being lost in the woods and leave while they have enough light to see where they're going. I like to pick a place near camp for late hunting so I can sit and watch until total darkness falls. Knowing the coun-

This is one of the first bulls I killed; now I pass up average-sized elk such as this.

try, I can find my way back to camp. If you're unsure about your trail, mark it with paper tissue. I always carry a flashlight in my pocket as well to help me find my way. I've shot some of my largest elk when there was barely enough light to see, and I've passed up a lot more because I was after a trophy or didn't want to bother with a smaller one. A prime time for elk to move is just as the last light is being washed off the mountains.

The recommended elk calibers will be discussed in the chapter on guns, but you should have a rifle that packs plenty of wallop. Elk are big and tough.

You'll discover how big they are when you have one laying on the ground. You won't believe the size! You probably won't be able to move the carcass unless you have help. One time, when Russell Tinsley and I were hunting in Colorado, I shot a medium-sized bull that fell in the shade. Russell wanted to move him into the sunlight to take pictures. We spent several lung-aching minutes shoving and pushing to nudge the carcass a few feet.

If you do shoot an elk, you'll have a problem getting it out of the woods. This is when the work begins. Even if you have access to a horse, you'll want to gut the elk immediately and prop it open where heat will escape and the carcass will begin to cool. You'll probably have to cut the animal in half so the horse can pack it out one piece at a time. This really is beneficial because elk have a tendency to spoil much more rapidly than deer, even in the cool mountain air, due to their size and thickness through the shoulders.

If I'm hunting where no horse is available, I won't be tempted to shoot even a lesser elk unless I can drive close to it in a four-wheel-drive pickup. I've back-packed out a few in pieces, and those are lessons you don't forget.

When I'm hunting alone, I carry lots of parachute cord and a little belt saw. I cut off the hindquarters and hang each one up before attending to the rest of the carcass. This not only lets the hindquarters start to cool, it eliminates a lot of the weight so you can better manage what is left.

Once the hindquarters are removed, I leave the carcass sprawled on one side and split the skin along the back. Then I peel the skin down the side to the middle of the belly. There is no need to gut the animal before you do this. To do so only makes things more difficult and messy. With the hide peeled down, the backbone, shoulder, ribs, and flank meat are exposed. The next step is to take off the shoulder and hang it. Then, starting at the neck, I remove the entire tenderloin. After that I cut away the flank meat, up to the rib cage, being careful not to puncture an intestine. I like to bone out the rest of the exposed side, hanging the meat in strips.

When this side is clean, I roll the carcass over and repeat the same procedure on the opposite side. After I'm through, the liver and heart are exposed and I save them if they're not damaged by bullets. While the meat cools and the blood dries, I take care of the head and cape. I skin up against the head as far as I can go, eliminating weight. The combination of antlers, head, and hide weighs more than some dressed deer.

If you get a bull elk down, you're going to find ruefully that elk hunting is not all fun and games. But after it's all over you're going to say it was worth it. A bull elk is a real prize, especially that first one.

Chapter 15

Challenging the Wary Whitetail

If you added all the hours I've spent pursuing deer, the total would equal at least a couple of years of my life. A trophy whitetail buck is the ultimate challenge. Among other factors, it takes age to grow bragging-sized antlers, and a buck doesn't live to be more than five or six years old by being dumb. Those less wary are killed before they have a chance to become trophies. To outwit a large-antlered buck, you have to be a little slicker than he is.

Nowadays, I try to get a bigger buck than any I've killed before, which means I do a whole lot of hunting but seldom any shooting. I've gone entire seasons without firing a shot. I don't intend to burden you with my standards; you have to work out in your own mind what's big enough.

But right off I should tell you that the only way to get a trophy buck is not to shoot a little one. If I'm simply looking for a deer to eat, I'll shoot a doe, if it's legal to take antlerless deer. It makes more sense to take a doe than a young buck. Give him the opportunity to grow up.

When you're after big deer, you have to make snap judgments. Sometimes you have only a split second to decide whether to shoot. Spend some time studying mounted deer heads. Notice how far

I passed up both these bucks; would you have shot the big one?

the antler beams extend beyond the ears. But the real test is in the woods. If you become a trophy hunter, you'll undoubtedly be dissatisfied with a few of the bucks you shoot. Antlers have a way of "shrinking" once a buck is on the ground.

One frosty-cold, early December day on the famous YO Ranch near Mountain Home, Texas, Winston and I rattled up probably two dozen bucks and didn't shoot one (I'll go into the rattling technique later). The YO has some nice bucks but not honest-to-goodness trophies, the kind you find down in the brush country of south Texas. So Winston and I rattled the bucks for our amusement, more than anything. But there were two or three that most any hunter would have been proud to hang on his wall.

The term *trophy* must be put in its proper perspective. Often its definition will depend on the general size of the deer in the area where you're hunting. A trophy in one place might be only an average buck in another.

But just because the buck lacks the groceries and the proper bloodlines to grow to record-book size, he isn't necessarily less crafty. No matter where you pursue him, a whitetail buck is one of—if not *the*—smartest animal on four feet.

Everything considered, successful deer hunting depends on the law of averages. The more time you spend in the woods, the better your chances are. A hunter might get lucky and shoot one big buck, but he won't take them with any consistency unless he knows what he's doing and stays with it.

I also believe in not making any disturbance in an area where you intend to hunt. If you're familiar with a place, don't go prowling through it right before the season. If work needs to be done, such as building or repairing tree stands, complete the job a month or two before the season, then stay out of the area until you're ready to hunt.

Have you ever wondered why you sometimes see the big bucks before the season, but they seem to vanish once hunting becomes legal? I know what can happen. I've driven around ranches a few days before the season and have seen quite a few deer. But the next time around on the same roads, I've sighted fewer. After several trips I'm lucky to see one. Whitetails catch on. They know when something is unnatural.

Unless they're chasing does during the rut, crafty old bucks aren't going to move around much in the daytime. If they do travel, they'll move away from human thoroughfares, such as roads. They know where the people are. In the thick thornbrush of south Texas, where I frequently hunt, deer travel through dense vegetation along ravines and washes. They never leave the thick cover, circling a clearing rather than going through it. They have my utmost respect; they're plenty savvy.

Most people hunt in the wrong places. They position themselves so they can watch a lot of country. While they might see some does and an occasional young buck, they'll never see deer with truly big bodies and antlers. You have to go back into the thick stuff, where visibility is limited, if you ever hope to get a glimpse of one. If I'm in a place where I'm not seeing any does, I figure my chances of seeing big buck are much better, and I've got the horns to prove this strategy works. Big bucks are furtive and like to stay away from other deer.

I like to hunt the offbeat places where other hunters don't go. I might have several blinds or stands, but I won't use some of them more than once a year. I like to hunt a different area each day; I want to keep the deer guessing just like they keep me guessing.

I hunt whenever I can, but when I'm trying to fine-tune a hunt, I pay particular attention to the moon phase and weather. One of my favorite times is when a quarter moon is visible in the afternoon. This occurs around the first-quarter phase of the moon. Deer come out earlier to browse during this time.

It amazes me how many hunters are unaware of the phases of the moon. While man's activities are dictated by daylight and the sun, the deer's routine revolves around the moon. They definitely start stirring when the moon comes up. Deer generally get up with the moon and go to bed with the moon.

Whitetails are often active just before and right after a weather change, especially if the temperature drops drastically. During the period just before a cold front comes through, it isn't uncommon to see deer moving all day long. But once the howling wind hits, the deer head for the protective thick stuff.

Deer also seem to like cold weather when there's a fine mist in the air. Something about the dampness juices them up. If the deer are about to rut, the combination of a temperature drop and a light rain puts the activity into high gear.

As with elk hunters, most deer hunters make the mistake of getting on their stands too late and leaving too early. I prefer to walk to my stand in total darkness. If possible, I'll be in the stand a full hour before legal shooting time. I'm going to make some disturbance even sneaking in, and I want to give the deer time to calm their nerves. Rather than leaving my stand in the afternoon, I stay until night has settled.

It's best to position your stand with the sun behind you, morning or evening. Even after the sun dies behind the western horizon, it leaves a glare that inhibits visibility. But sometimes circumstances such as wind direction force you to look into the glare, and you have to adapt the best you can.

I recall how I once adapted. I was hunting near my home and I knew what direction the deer would come from to enter our oat field and feed at night. Because of a neighbor's fence, I was forced to look in one direction, directly toward the dying sun. I heard deer coming, their hooves crunching dry post oak leaves which had fallen in the trail, but because of the combination of twilight and glare along the horizon, I couldn't see anything. I'd been standing behind a tree and watching. I got down and rolled on one side so the deer would be silhouetted against the sky as they passed—and I was able to pick the biggest buck out of the bunch.

Deer like to move into their feeding grounds at dusk; that's why it's important not to give up too early. Also, if you move and disturb them, you're going to make them suspicious or actually spook them. They'll change their routines and your future chances at that spot will be reduced. That's why I like to hunt different areas each day; it keeps the deer off guard.

As I stated in the chapter on elk, I'm primarily an ambush hunter. In most places, depending on the terrain, your best bet is to sit quietly and look. Let the deer move about and make the mistakes, rather than the other way around. Try to learn everything you can about your quarry: where he's feeding, bedding, and traveling. Understand that deer prowl around just before and after a weather change, but otherwise they like to move real early and real late in the day, with some additional movement around midday. A buck doesn't get in his bed and stay there all day. He likes to get up occasionally to stretch his muscles. He often moves around briefly at the height of the day, when the woods are quiet. He knows when the hunters are in their camp.

So stay in the woods as much as you can. Expose yourself to deer. That's the way to get a buck. You won't find any while lounging around camp. If you want to rest and take things easy, stay at home. It saves time and money.

Dub Martin of Des Allemands, Louisiana, likes to blow on a deer call while sitting on a stand, and he's called hundreds of deer to him. Dub has had much more success than I have because I depend more on rattling than on a mouth-blown call. In my home state of Texas it's illegal to use a mouth-blown deer call while hunting, although I've called quite a few this way when taking pictures. Under Texas law it's legal to call deer by rattling antlers together. You can even bait the deer with feed like corn, but you can't use a mouth-blown call. Why the law is contradictory, I don't know. Can you figure that rationale?

Dub has confidence in the call because he's had success with it. Confidence in your call is important, no matter what the hunting technique. I've received letters from people all over who've called deer. H.M. Mills III of Athens, Georgia, said he called 18 whitetails into bow range during one season. Brian C. Wells of Washington, D.C., reported that "although I was hunting an area known as unproductive woods for deer, I managed to call four whitetails close enough to take shots at three of the four." Gary Thomas of Newport, Ohio, said he took a deer call into the woods to see if it would work—"And it did!" Alex Delano of Ithaca, New York, told me he "called in and killed a nice eight-point buck on opening day of deer season. I shot him at a range of 20 yards. A doe also came to the call just before the buck."

As with any call, the response to a deer call tends to be erratic and unpredictable. Calling seems to produce best when deer are generally undisturbed, in an area of minimal hunting pressure or during early archery seasons.

There are a couple of basic calls. Deer communicate in soft bleats. The buck makes a low bleat and the doe answers with a soft bleat. Imitating the bleat will bring a buck to you. The other call is a deer distress sound, which often attracts deer in a hurry.

The deer respond almost too fast at times—like what happened the day I was demonstrating deer calling to Tom Hayes and Russell Tinsley, both of whom have authored popular books on hunting whitetails. They were curious as to whether calling would really work.

Notice the mistake here? I've got my rifle slung over my shoulder instead of where I can get to it quicker and easier. It pays to be prepared.

It was up in the morning and I had them climb into a platform tree blind. I stayed on the ground, sitting with my back against the tree, right in the middle of a trail. I began wailing on the deer call.

Tom and Russell were where they could immediately see the

deer, a doe coming at full speed. She never slowed. It happened so fast that the first I saw of her was when she rounded a bend in the trail, which put her almost on me. For an instant all I could see were ears and eyeballs. I don't know which of us was the most startled. When I saw the doe I moved—or almost jumped—and she saw the movement and veered off into the brush, crashing her way through. I know that incident taught me a lesson; I won't sit in a trail anymore.

As I've recommended before, get an instruction record or tape and practice the calling sounds at home. Producing any calling sound isn't all that difficult. You only need to work at it a spell.

But while a deer call attracts, it also can have the opposite effect. When I'm driving deer, I like to blow on a call as I walk along. The sound will make deer move out when nothing else will.

Sometimes a buck will almost refuse to move. As drivers walk through his territory, he'll double back between the hunters or simply lay still and hide until the humans pass by—sometimes only a few yards away, as Gene Hornbeck, outdoor editor of the *Omaha World Herald*, found out. I was hunting with Gene and several others northwest of Burwell in central Nebraska. We were making a drive along the Calamus River. I was standing up on the river bank where I could see ahead as Gene and other drivers fought their way through high dead weeds and thick brush. I heard Gene shoot and almost instantly saw a 10-point buck bound into view. He jumped into the river and swam to a small island where I was able to shoot him. Later, Gene told he approached within seven yards of the buck's hiding place before the animal panicked and flushed. He took a snap shot but he didn't have much of a chance.

Even the deer call I manufacture is no magic cure for your hunting ills. It's a tool, nothing more. Its effectiveness depends on how and where you use it. The fundamentals of good hunting still apply. Scout to find where deer are ranging, keep the wind to your face as you move into your hunting territory, and remain quiet and motionless on your stand. Don't believe that malarkey about deer not looking up. If you move at the wrong time, a sharp-eyed deer will spot you as readily in a tree stand as it will if you're on the ground. When deer learn that a tree stand is associated with danger, they'll look at it suspiciously every time they go by. Whitetails have nerves wound as tight as a watchspring, and they're ready to spook at the slightest excuse.

If the deer go into heat and the rut begins, you can forget about any rules of deer behavior. It's a whole new ballgame.

The rut is the time to catch a trophy buck with his guard down. He won't be nearly as alert. The sexual urge scrambles his usually ultrasensitive defense. If he's going to make a mistake this is when he'll usually make it.

When the rut is underway, you won't find me in the woods without my rattling horns slung over a shoulder. I've rattled my share of bucks—large and small—and each experience is unique. Different deer have different personalities and they react to rattling in different ways.

I saw the two extremes the morning I tried to rattle a buck for Russell Tinsley. Although Texans call it "horn rattling," that is just imaginative vernacular since a deer has antlers, not horns. But, what the heck? Rattling is nothing more than banging antlers together to simulate bucks fighting.

The December morning dawned frosty and clear, ideal for rattling. We eased quietly into position along the slope of a small hill before dawn. Yelping coyotes greeted the new day as the horizon behind us began to brighten.

Blurry objects gradually came into focus. In this sprawl of deep south Texas, near the Mexico border, there's a certain sameness, a seemingly endless view of low-slung thornbrush and cacti. But looks are deceiving. The mineral-rich soil produces plants high in protein, which in turn grow exceptional deer. This region has accounted for more than its share of Boone and Crockett Club heads.

When the light was sufficient to see for some distance, I adjusted my gloves and picked up the rattling horns. I normally wear gloves when rattling. Catch a cold, numb finger between the horns as you bang them together and you'll never again forget to wear gloves.

I hit the antlers together two or three times and almost immediately saw the deer coming. He was running, and running hard. Even at a distance I could tell this was not your ordinary deer; he had the body of a Hereford bull.

The cagey old-timer didn't charge right on in. About 150 yards

When I hit the antlers together, this buck came bounding out of the underbrush.

away he abruptly applied the brakes, head held high, massive antlers outlined against the sky.

I waited impatiently for Russell to shoot. I almost was tempted to holler, "Come on, come on!"

The deer stood there only a second or two, then wheeled and took off as fast as he had arrived. With a few quick bounds he disappeared into the thick brush.

I was shaking from excitement. "What happened, why didn't you shoot?" I asked.

Russell was dejected and rightfully so. "I blew it," he admitted. "He was standing partly behind a leafless mesquite bush, but I had a reasonable shot. I just hoped for a better one, thinking he'd step on out into the open."

Remember this piece of advice: When you're deer hunting and you get a reasonable shot, take it. That usually will be the best shot you'll get. A second chance is a rare luxury.

Later that morning, about a half mile away, we hid on the side of a small hill—or just a high place in the flat terrain—and I rattled while we watched a large flat below covered with prickly pear cactus. By my watch I rattled for 45 minutes. I was ready to move to another place but, as is my hunter's habit, I slowly turned my head and looked around before getting up. Across the flat, almost casually, came a buck at a half trot. I nudged Russell and whispered, "There's your buck."

The deer was no more than 75 yards away when a 6mm slug hit him behind the shoulder and dropped him on the spot. The eight-point buck had heavy, high antlers. While his rack couldn't compare with the one we saw earlier, this was a buck worth bragging about just the same.

Those two bucks displayed exactly opposite mannerisms. The first one came fast, running; the second was more deliberate, sneaking, taking his time.

One of the largest whitetails I've ever killed was on that same ranch. I was in one of the high-rise towers familiar to the south Texas scene, where no trees of substance can be found for building tree stands. A typical tower is 10 to 12 feet high, a boxlike structure sitting on legs, with guy wires holding it in place so it won't topple in a high wind.

I saw the deer coming from a long way off, or I should say I saw antlers. That's all that was visible above the brush, just a pair of huge antlers seemingly floating along. When the buck was about 500 yards away he stopped in a small opening and I figured that was it, my only chance. I rested the rifle, took a shot, and missed. At that range the deer didn't even know he'd been shot at.

I rattled this buck in the rough Texas country near Del Rio on the Mexico border.

He ambled back into the brush. I was afraid he was leaving, so I picked up my rattling horns, and banged them together hard. The buck turned and here he came. I could tell that he had me located; so when he was about 150 yards away, passing through a narrow clearing, I dropped him.

What I did, a lot of people said couldn't be done, that is, rattling a buck from a tower blind. That's bull. I've rattled many out of such blinds. But when I'm up high like that I do alter my rattling style. I rattle only now and then, spending more time looking than rattling. I rattle for a few seconds, then lay the horns aside and use my binoculars to study all the area around me. After a few minutes, I rattle briefly again. I rattle sporadically like this because I don't want the buck to zero in on where the sound is coming from, and I don't want him to catch any movement.

Rattling deer adds a whole new dimension to hunting. While it's become known as a Texas method, I'm convinced it'll work on whitetails in the rut no matter where you find them. I've received letters from hunters who've rattled deer in many states and even in Canadian provinces.

Rattling really is pretty simple. There's no "right" way to do it because no two deer make the same sounds when they're fighting. As with a deer call, it's how and where you try that counts.

Some people say it can't be done, but I've rattled many bucks out of a platform blind like this in south Texas.

All you need is a pair of antlers. I like a pair of some substance, with eight or 10 points, because the sound of heavy antlers banging together carries farther. But I don't think size is that critical; almost any antlers will do, even mule deer antlers.

Cut the antlers from the skull. To avoid sticking yourself accidentally, you might want to saw off the tips of the tines as well as completely remove the brow tines or so-called "dog catchers." Take a rasp to the rough bases to make them more comfortable to hold (but still wear gloves). Drill a small hole through either antler, about a half inch from the base, and attach them with a cord or leather thong about 18 inches long. You can sling them over your shoulder for easy transport. If you use antlers you picked up in the woods or off a deer that has been in storage for some time, soak them overnight in water or linseed oil to restore the natural sound. Dry antlers have more of a high, hollow ring.

To get some idea of the technique, we offer an instruction cassette. But you can't go wrong no matter how you do it. The idea is to simulate two bucks in combat. Another buck hears the melee and comes to the scene either to whip the victor of the fight and claim the spoils or to steal away with the doe or breed her while the others are preoccupied. It isn't unusual, if an area has a high buck-doe ratio, for one or more young bucks to trail an older buck and his lady friend around; they aren't strong enough physically to challenge the chief so they stand around hoping for a break. When they hear the fake fight, they think that break has arrived. It isn't uncommon to rattle two or three small bucks almost simultaneously.

Timing is more important than the sound. The buck must have his sexual drive going. Also, the sound should reach a buck looking for a doe and not actually with one, although I've seen bucks leave does to come to rattling.

A prime period is just before the rut goes into full swing. The bucks get ready before the does. They make scrapes and leave calling cards and wait around for something to happen. This is when they are eager, sparring about, either hooking brush or trying to pick a fight with another buck.

But whitetails can't read the rules. I've had hunters tell me you can't rattle bucks in south Texas until after mid-December. I've rattled many before that. The largest buck my son, Hunter, has

When rattling, I like to use heavy antlers.

killed was one I rattled during the Thanksgiving weekend. You might rattle a buck even if the "chemistry" isn't right. Animal calling is an imprecise thing. About the only certainty is the uncertainty.

I'm convinced that some deer come to rattling more from curiosity than anything. But one thing's for certain: you'll never rattle anything unless you get in the woods and try.

Learn to look for and recognize scrapes. You'll usually find them along the edges of clearings. These are bare, pawed-out patches of ground under overhanging limbs that the buck can reach. When a buck regularly visits a scrape, he'll mouth and nibble at the leaves and twigs. If a doe finds the scrape and urinates on the torn ground, that's the signal she's ready and the rut is on. The buck "stakes out" his territory with a series of scrapes, and if another buck comes along, he either puts up or shuts up.

Scrapes indicate sexual activity. At least you know a buck is in the general area. But if you can't locate a scrape, simply move from one spot to another, rattling as you go. If you're hunting during the rut, you always have a chance of duping a buck into rifle range.

As for the best time to rattle, I prefer the period from dawn until past sunrise, although I have rattled deer in late afternoon. If the deer really are running, you can rattle them all day long.

Some hunters bang the antlers together a few times, then beat on the brush and the ground. I don't think all these added sound effects are necessary, but no harm is done throwing them in. Find a rattling style you feel comfortable with and stay with it. Getting confidence in the technique takes time. You won't rattle a buck every time you try.

When preparing to rattle, conceal yourself with good visibility all around, particularly downwind. If you're hunting with a buddy, get back to back, so you can watch both ways with a minimum of movement. No matter which direction a buck might come from, he'll almost invariably circle the sound before departing. As you rattle, turn your head slowly, avoiding any jerky movements, and watch and listen. If you pause periodically to listen, sometimes you'll hear the hoofbeats of a deer approaching before you actually see him.

That will get your attention, I guarantee.

Chapter 16

Muleys Aren't Dumb

If you trust what you've heard, the mule deer is the most dumb-witted member of the deer family, at least when compared with the whitetail. Don't you believe it. An old muley is plenty savvy. You never see most of the big bucks. If you flush a big buck from his hiding place while scouting, you won't find him there again. He'll move to another place where you're less likely to jump him. He'll find a place where he can see or hear everything approaching, and he won't move unless he feels threatened.

A crafty old west Texas desert mule deer showed me how tricky a buck can be. I was standing at the edge of a canyon with my rifle slung over my shoulder, looking through binoculars. It was mid-morning and I'd removed my jacket. A bright sun in a clear blue sky reflected off the rimrocks, generating plenty of solar heat even for late November.

No, I wasn't hunting. I was play-acting. Russell Tinsley had located this canyon earlier and decided it would be a scenic place for some photographs. It was deep and filled with brush. Far below, the sun-bleached rocks in the dry creek bed shimmered in the light. Several miles away, the Rio Grande was just a ribbon of dark blue.

When we had returned to the camp house after hunting that morning, Russell asked if we could go to the canyon to take some hunting-scene pictures. Of course I unloaded my rifle before getting in the Jeep.

If you believe that bunk about a mule deer being dumb, you'll probably never get one like this in your rifle sight. (Photo by Erwin A. Bauer.)

For about 15 minutes, maybe longer, we'd moved back and forth along the canyon rim to change the angle of the light. I was casually peering through the fieldglasses, trying to act as though I was hunting, when I was startled by a commotion. No more than 75 yards down the canyon slope, brush rattled as a wide-antlered buck burst into view, bouncing away in that familiar pogo-stick-like gait. He angled down into the canyon, turned along the creek bed, and ran out of sight. With an unloaded rifle, I was helpless to do anything.

Imagine, that old rascal had hidden right there with us moving about and talking. I guess finally his nerves couldn't take it, so he figured he'd better leave.

But that buck did something else he wasn't supposed to do, according to some people. A whitetail deer, it's been said, will come out of hiding at full speed and won't slow down until it's over the next ridge or two, but a mule deer has the habit of stopping to look back. This buck we jumped from the canyon didn't pause. If you wait for a mule deer to stop, you might never get a shot. Sometimes it will stop, but often it won't. You can't stand around and wait for something to happen; you have to make it happen.

The largest mule deer I've killed was a fine example. I was sitting where I could watch a trail coming out of the Colorado high country. Hunter activity often pushes mule deer out of an area before they're really ready to leave.

I'd been sitting and watching for five hours. Somehow, this buck slipped by me. I don't know how, because I'm an alert watcher. But when I first saw him, he was about 700 yards away. Even at that distance, I could see his rack through my fieldglasses.

This is the whopper I chased for miles in the Colorado high country.

When migrating, mule deer adopt a steady gait—alternating walking and trotting—and stick with it. They can cover a lot of country in a short time.

Sighting the buck so far away, it would have been easy to have given him a parting gesture and hollered goodbye. But I never hesitated; at least I was willing to try to make something happen. I jumped off the big rock I'd been sitting on and gave chase, running to another ridge a half mile away, maybe farther. I looked through the binoculars and saw the deer cross a saddle and turn to the left. This turned out to be a rare stroke of luck. The buck went about a half mile before angling downhill again. If he hadn't taken this detour, I probably never would have seen him again. By the time he picked up another migration trail, I'd halved the distance between us. This was my lucky day. By happenstance, where the trails forked, I took the same trail he was traveling. I kept running until I glimpsed him again, just as he was getting ready to disappear into some thick juniper. He was crossing a small gully and was coming out the opposite side. He was about 200 yards away, and I had only one chance. My nerves were shot and I was heaving from exhaustion, but somehow I found him in the 2½ x 8 variable scope with tapered crosshairs and dropped him with a 7mm Magnum slug.

I didn't realize how big he really was until I walked up to him. He had a huge body and antlers to match; a 37.5-inch outside antler spread and 21 points. By the odometer of the pickup, it was two miles from the rock to where the chase ended, but I'd traveled a zig-zag path and probably had run more than twice that far.

That trophy was the culmination of six days of hard hunting and some determined long-distance running. I'd turned down several smaller bucks. And I was in top physical condition. Otherwise, I couldn't have made it that far in such a short time in the thin mountain air, where it takes effort to walk, much less run.

When there's hunting pressure, some bucks, like this one, decide to depart for more sedate surroundings. Others hide. I once sat on a rocky ridge in west Colorado and watched mule deer bed down on a slope across the way. When other hunters came by, the deer stayed where they were, not moving, or kept a thicket between themselves and the hunters until the hunters passed by. Some old bucks don't leave high country until the snow is belly deep; they stay along the edge of cliffs and lower benches and you can't get close to them.

But normally when an army of hunters moves into the woods, many of the deer leave. Activity as well as weather will make them move. I like to locate a trail leaving the high country, then get on

It pays to spend your time hunting; my son Hunter bagged this buck while I was breaking camp.

it and watch. The odds are that, sooner or later, a good buck will come by.

When watching a trail, the payoff might take minutes, hours, or even days. You've got to stay on the trail and remain alert. You'd be surprised how easily a deer can get by, like that big buck got past me. If mule deer are migrating, you might see one at any time of day.

Some years after that incident, my son, Hunter, and I were in the same area where I shot the trophy buck. We'd hunted for four days without seeing anything worth shooting. While I was breaking camp I suggested that Hunter go to the next level, about 1,000 feet higher, and watch. We'd found deer sign there the previous day, which shows the value of scouting even when you are actually hunting.

Hunter was sitting, watching a game trail, when right at noon, a large-antlered buck came around a bend in the trail. Hunter shot him. The buck had a 31-inch outside spread (27 inches inside) and five points (10 total points, Eastern count).

This proves, among other things, that you're not going to kill any deer unless you're in the woods with them. And you have to know the country. If Hunter hadn't been sitting where he was— above the trail so he had good visibility—he would've spooked the deer before he got a chance to shoot.

The advantage a local outfitter has over a hunter who's unfamiliar with the country is that he knows where to go. Mule deer are funny; good numbers of them may be in one area, while over the next ridge there are none. They go where the food is.

Me, I'd rather hunt on my own. This is the only way you'll learn anything. You can't depend on others; you have to reason things out yourself.

When Winston and I first went to Colorado, in 1952, we got there a week before the season started. We stopped at every sporting goods store and looked up game wardens, asking anyone who might know about places to hunt. One contact led to another until finally we were put in touch with an old-timer who had horses to rent and who also, for a fee, packed game out of the woods. Since he wanted to pack out any deer we killed, he told us about a choice spot.

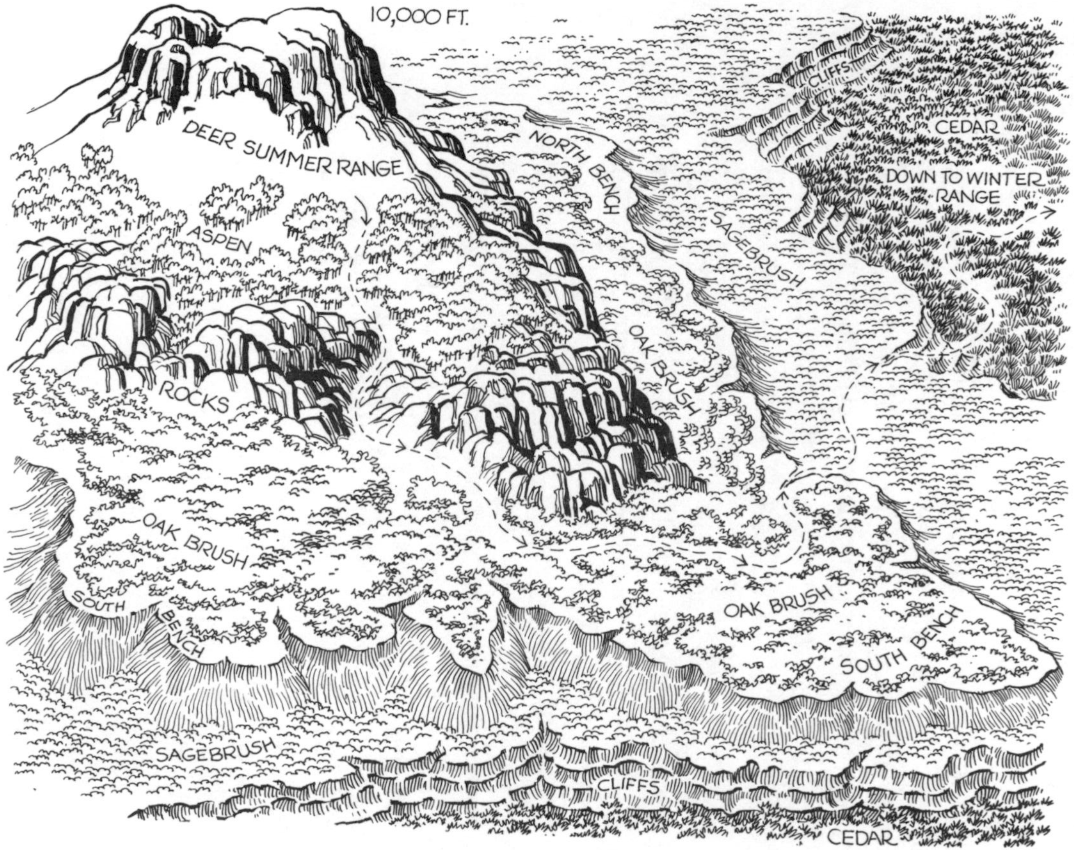
10,000 FT.
DEER SUMMER RANGE
NORTH BENCH
CLIFFS
CEDAR
DOWN TO WINTER RANGE
ASPEN
SAGEBRUSH
OAK BRUSH
ROCKS
OAK BRUSH
SOUTH BENCH
OAK BRUSH
SOUTH BENCH
SAGEBRUSH
CLIFFS
CEDAR

This is a drawing of one of my favorite Colorado hunting spots, where I've shot several big bucks. I wait in ambush at the base of the rocky cliff where a migration trail comes from the high summer range into the lower oak brush country.

He said we should go up the mountain, about four miles above where we were camped. It was a torturous hike, all uphill, but worth it. He explained that we should sit where migration trails came out of the country higher up. The higher country was accessible by road, he said, and lots of hunters went there.

"They'll run the deer out of there to you," he pointed out. "Let the other hunters do the work."

That was the first time I learned that hunter pressure will move deer as readily as stormy weather. The limit then was two bucks per hunter and Winston and I had no problems filling our quota. All four bucks were in the trophy class.

The hunt was not only productive but educational. I learned the value of being in top physical condition. I also learned about proper boot fit; when I got back to Texas I had blisters on the end of my toes from walking down steep grades, and I hobbled around for weeks.

But you never quit learning. For about 20 years running, Winston and I never missed a Colorado season. If we didn't find the buck we wanted in the early archery season or the regular October season, we'd go back for the special December hunts, held where there were too many deer for the winter range. On one of these hunts, I didn't have sun shades and I almost went snow blind.

During these two decades we called a lot of deer, using the deer call with distress cries during the October season. One time I called and Winston shot a buck with 16 total points, an honest-to-goodness trophy. We were calling in thick timber—a mixture of aspens, spruce, and scrub oak. We knew it was a good area because we found buck rubs on saplings and there were numerous deer beds.

We would call, then go 300 yards, actually stepping the distance off, and call again. In thick cover, deer can't hear a call much farther away than that, and we found that if we went more than 300 yards, we'd spook the deer from their beds. At one stop, we'd been calling about 15 minutes when this big buck came sneaking through the brush. He was only 25 yards away when Winston shot him.

Winston and I also did a lot of calling during the earlier archery seasons, and while we called many deer close, we never got one to come as close as the one Lynn Willis did. He and his wife, Bettye,

I was standing out in the open when I called this doe close.

were hunting together, separated by a few yards, arrows nocked
and ready. Lynn blew on a deer call. He heard the thumping sound
of a running deer, and before he knew what was happening a doe
was right on top of him—literally. Lynn grabbed the doe's nose
and held on as the deer thrashed about. Bettye ran to where they
were wrestling and Lynn, from the corner of his eye, saw her raise
her bow to shoot. Lynn started screaming for her not to shoot.
Knowing something about the accuracy of Bettye's shooting, I
couldn't blame him. With Lynn hollering, the deer got frightened,
pulled loose, jumped to her feet, and took off.

You can call deer in more open country while the animals are
out and about in early morning just at daybreak. I like early better
than late because I believe the deer are more interested in getting
something to eat in late afternoon.

But if you attempt to call during the day, you have to get in the
thick stuff where deer bed. In the mountains this generally will be
on the north slopes and benches where there are shady areas. If
you're hunting with a buddy, sit back to back so one hunter can
watch downwind. No two deer will react alike; some are eager,

others are sneaky. Stay at least 15 minutes in one place before moving on.

If the deer aren't moving or won't come to a call, watch a waterhole around noon. Some of the best deer hunting is missed because hunters are in camp at midday. Deer often move around noon when it's quiet. They can't lay in their beds all day; they need to

This is a scene on my west Texas ranch where both whitetails and desert mule deer are found.

get up and stretch. But they'll be in the thick stuff, so you have to be in there with them to see them.

Some people like to walk and hunt, but they normally hunt too fast. If you do walk, spend more time looking than walking. One December, Winston and I were hunting the sagebrush country near Dove Creek, in an area where there was a special season to reduce an overpopulation of deer. We had walked to a ridge and were glassing a far-off snow-covered slope. We watched for 10 or 15 minutes before slight movement gave the buck away. He was bedded behind a bush, and all that could be seen was the top of his antlers. As he turned his head we saw the antlers move. But he was in a position where there was no chance to get at him.

The trouble with walking is that an old buck is too sharp. He'll either hear or see the hunter. It's better to find a much-traveled trail and watch. Let other hunters move deer by you. If you're in an area with few other hunters, you can drive mule deer, just as you drive whitetails. Mule deer generally will stick to trails. But you must know the lay of the land and escape trails to know where to wait in ambush. If I'm doing the driving, I blow on the deer call to move the deer out.

Once a mule deer gets on a trail, it'll be reluctant to leave it. Thanks to that behavior, I was able to get a trophy with a 30-inch spread and 14 points, a perfect match on both sides, every long point forked. I've never seen another mule deer with such a symmetrical rack.

With any kind of luck, brother Winston or Russell Tinsley would have gotten him. They saw him first. But he'd come down the escape trail and somehow slipped past them. They didn't see him until he was 500 yards away. They opened up with their rifles. One shot connected, spinning the deer around. That put him on a run and he dashed down the trail, but obviously slowed shortly when he figured he was safe.

I was hidden about a half mile down the trail. Russell told me later that exactly 30 minutes after he and Winston had shot, he heard a shot from my direction. The bullet that had hit the buck earlier only grazed the rump, taking off hair without breaking the skin. But even after being hit and frightened, the deer stayed on the trail and I got him.

Brother Winston and Russell Tinsley got the first crack at this buck, but I ended up getting him on down the trail.

That might sound like the mule deer is indeed dumb. But, really, just because a mule deer habitually follows a trail doesn't make it any less wise to the tricks of survival.

While we were working on this book, Russell and I took a break to do some mule deer hunting out in west Texas, beyond the Pecos River, in rough country of rimrocks and deep washes. I was watching two mule deer, a doe and forkhorn buck, browsing in sparse brush not far away. They were casually going about their business when suddenly they threw their heads up, ears cupped alertly. Then I heard it; Russell was coming toward me. He was several hundred yards off but rocks clinked as he walked. It's difficult to walk in this country of loose rocks without making noise, and sound carries for a long distance. The deer listened briefly, but then, before Russell came into sight, they turned and bounded off, disappearing into the canyon, not stopping to look back.

Yeah, mule deer are dumb—about as dumb as a fox.

Chapter 17

Black Bear Encounters

I knew the bear was exceptional, but I didn't realize how big he really was until we tried to load him into the pickup. It took three of us, all reaching back for a little extra, to push and pull the carcass into the bed. Gary Calhoun estimated that this male black bear, just out of hibernation, weighed 500 pounds. He said it would've weighed nearly 600 in the fall after putting on some fat.

Only after I'd eased up on the bear and poked him with the rifle barrel to be sure he was dead did I get excited. Before that, there wasn't time. Everything had happened too suddenly.

The sun had vanished behind distant mountaintops and the Colorado air was chilly. I zipped my jacket and continued the vigil. After four hours of sitting and watching, I should have been disspirited, but I wasn't. I knew that if a bear did show, it probably would be just at dark.

I was right. The grove of quakies was quiet and it seemed as though someone were slowly turning a rheostat switch, reducing the light from bright to dim. The only sound was the hum of mosquitoes. As twilight settled through the aspens, I saw movement, or at least I thought I did. Maybe my eyes were playing tricks. I squinted up the trail.

The lumbering shape looked like a box car. As I brought the Model 600 Remington rifle up, the bear turned slightly to the left. I put the crosshairs of the scope just behind his ribs and touched

A .308 slug dropped this big Colorado bear on the spot.

'er off. The .308 slug ploughed into the chest cavity and the bear was dead before he hit the ground.

This was my eighth black bear and by far the largest. I've passed up a dozen or more because they weren't large enough. I won't shoot another one unless I find a bear bigger than the 500 pounder, which probably means I probably won't shoot another. The odds of finding one larger are remote, especially since I don't hunt bear all that often. To get the trophies you have to dedicate yourself.

The only problem with that jumbo I got in the Colorado mountains was that while it had a tremendous body, it didn't have a head to match. The head was stubby. Outfitter Chuck Davies told me if the head had been long and angular, typical for the species, the bear easily would have qualified for the Boone and Crockett Club record book. As it was, the bear missed by only a half inch.

I shot that bear in the spring while watching a bait. If that sounds unsporting, it's obvious you've never tried it. One of my companions on the hunt was Jim Zumbo, author of *Hunting America's Mule Deer*. Jim told me of his frustrations while trying to shoot a bear in New Brunswick, in the thick forests along the Miramichi River.

"For three years in a row I had bear approach my stand," he said, "But none gave me an opportunity for a shot. In every case all I saw was a patch of black in the brush. I learned to respect bears. I also found that baiting is not a surefire way to kill a bear, and indeed is a sporting way to hunt."

The black bear is much sharper than most people give it credit for being. (Photo by Stocke Stockebrand.)

Various baits can be used for bears. When I hunted in Ontario, I watched garbage dumps at a deserted logging camp. Our party made other baits from suckers that we seined from small creeks that originated in lakes where the fish were spawning. Any carrion will do. The greater the stench, the more appeal a bait seems to have.

Gary Calhoun of Grand Junction baits at his Colorado hunting camp with animal waste he gets from a slaughterhouse. He dumps at least three 55-gallon drums of offal at each bait station. The same stations are maintained year after year. Once bears learn where the bait is and become accustomed to the locations, they return to check the stations each spring.

If you wish to try to bait a bear on your own, read the laws of the state where you are hunting to make sure it's legal. Some states have special regulations. In Wisconsin, for example, it's illegal to bait with meat and honey.

But getting a bear to come to a bait doesn't guarantee the makings of a bearskin rug. Black bears are basically nocturnal, and they're seldom seen except very early or late in the day.

Even if a bear comes to a bait, it'll remain suspicious. As eyesight goes, the bear's would rank as only average, but its hearing and nose are superb. Since bait watching is ambush hunting, the most critical consideration is wind direction. Human scent will put terror into any wild animal.

I like to think I outsmarted that trophy I got in Colorado. If I'd stayed where I first sat down that day I never would've gotten the bear. When the wind changed, I changed positions. I didn't want my scent blowing over the bait or toward the trail leading to it.

Wind currents are always tricky in the mountains, but they're particularly so during thundershowers. You've got to stay alert. As I moved around, I picked a stinky hog skin off the bait and dragged it behind me to cover my scent.

Fresh tracks indicated that one or more bears were visiting each bait station regularly, but two members of our party watched baits for four straight days and never saw a bear. I only can speculate that the bears either came in after dark, or the hunters got impatient and careless, or both, which was probably the case.

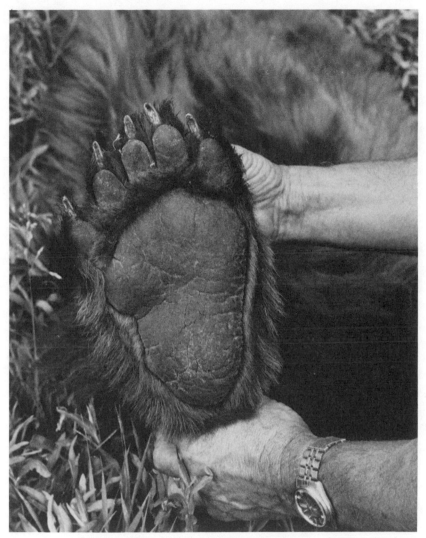

Imagine what kind of track a paw this size leaves.

When a hunter moves into position to watch a bait, he wants to keep the breeze in his face and not walk around where he doesn't have to. Human odor can linger for a long time. If you hunt both morning and evening, I'd recommend watching different baits, because you're going to leave some human scent behind.

I think the best time to hunt is during the dark of the moon,

Fred Bear (right) got his bear with bow and arrow and I shot mine with a rifle during our Ontario hunt.

when bears can't feed through the night. Even so, be especially alert just at daybreak and again at twilight. This is when a bear is most likely to show.

While hunting near Sudbury, Ontario, Fred Bear and I went at it a bit differently. A bush pilot flew Fred and me to a deserted logging camp. These remote camps operate when the lakes are frozen, but they shut down once the ice thaws.

When the loggers leave, bears move in, raiding the garbage dumps. Fred and I were hunting near a lake in heavy spruce, birch, and poplar timber. We'd pussyfoot to where we could peek at a garbage dump and, more often than not, a bear would be digging there, so intent on what it was doing that it became careless. Both Fred and I turned down bears until we found the ones we wanted. Fred got a large male with bow and arrow and I got one of about the same size with a rifle.

Fred has used a bow and arrow to shoot about every species of big game found in the world, but he told me his favorite game animal was a bear.

"Each bear has a distinct personality and no two react alike,"

Fred said. "And a bear is as challenging as any game animal you are going to find."

Those Ontario bears were coal black, but the pelts of those in Colorado are more reddish, pale brown and creamy. The colors of bears can vary widely from region to region.

Baiting is just one way to hunt black bears. They're also hunted with dogs. Hunters chase after the dogs on horseback. Pot-shooting a treed bear isn't my idea of sport, and I'm also not too wild about horseback riding since with working on a ranch I've had plenty to harden my knees. So you know how I stand on that matter.

I've also hunted bears in the fall, using the same techniques I use when ambush-hunting mule deer. I scout until I find where bears are feeding, then I locate a trail with fresh sign going to the food source and I get on the trail and wait. But if you're impatient, this method isn't for you. Sometimes you might watch a trail and not see a bear for days, if ever. Bears don't always cooperate as you think they should.

Black bears love mountain berries and scrub-oak acorns found in the high country of the Western states. You can easily identify where they've been feeding by broken limbs and leaves littered on the ground. A bear isn't very tidy.

As when hunting elk or mule deer, stay on the trail until total darkness. Sometimes a bear puts in an appearance so late in the day that you can see only a dark blob moving through the timber. I always use a scope sight because you can still see to shoot long after iron sights blur and become worthless.

Of the eight bears I've shot, all but two were in late afternoon, after sundown. But of all the bears I've seen, including those I've passed up, I would imagine equal numbers were spotted early and late in the day. But if you're going to get on a trail for a morning hunt, get there long before daylight, sneaking in quietly with the wind to your advantage. You don't want to let the bear know you're anywhere around. The element of surprise is the hunter's best friend.

Although I've sneaked up on bears and ambushed them, I've never called one, the main reason being I've never taken the challenge on as a project. I have no doubt that if I wanted to call a bear, I could. It's been done.

I got this bear and mule deer buck on the same October hunt in Colorado.

Dad called quite a few bears in Vermejo Park in northern New Mexico. He brought them in with rabbit distress cries he made by squeaking with his lips. But a deer call or short-range predator call will also do the job. Dad wasn't intentionally trying to call bears; he was calling bobcats but brought in black bears instead. I've also heard from many hunters, from California to Maine, who've called bears.

Calling a bear is not unlike calling any other wild animal. You've got to get into the bear's range, find where his daily routine takes him, and stay after him. It's a matter of organization and planning.

Chapter 18

Rattlesnake Hunting

Hunting is my vocation but it's also my hobby. Our business is at a peak in the winter, and February is a busy month for me because I have to catch up with work I ignored earlier while deer hunting and calling varmints. Having been trapped inside for a month or longer, come March I've got a good case of cabin fever. It's the time of year when there isn't much to do, except go rattlesnake hunting. I enjoy hunting the deadly reptiles and bringing them back alive. It's an exciting sport that keeps you jumping—literally, if you see a rattler slithering near your feet.

I've heard criticism of this practice. Some people say rattlesnakes provide a beneficial service by eating rodents. Maybe so, but I'd just as soon leave that job to nonpoisonous snakes. There's a market for rattlesnakes, and I consider them to be like fur-bearing animals—a renewable resource. But I also hunt them to remove a health hazard. I regularly find rattlers near my ranch house and at my mother's house a short distance away. We'd just as soon not have them around, thank you.

Rattlers caught live can be sold for medical research, for display purposes such as snake exhibits, or for their hides to be made into hatbands and belts. But hunting isn't going to have much impact on the overall population. I don't care how good a snake hunter you are, you're going to get only a small percentage; you're not going to find all the dens. And nature has a way of replenishing

This is the kind of country where I like to hunt rattlesnakes.

the supply, a female rattler having three to 14 young. The abundance or lack of snakes in an area depends on available food, as with any wildlife.

Unlike some places where a rattlesnake or two might find winter sanctuary in an earthen burrow, compliments of an armadillo or ground squirrel, rattlers in the rough-rock country of Texas where I hunt gang up in rocky caverns to hibernate. The most inconspicuous looking hole in a hillside might yield a couple dozen, maybe more.

Sometimes a lot more. I remember a den Winston and I located near the town of Sweetwater, known for its annual rattlesnake roundup. A huge rock about 15 feet in diameter lay on top of another. One side of the rock sandwich backed up to a dirt bank and between the layers were many crevices. We gassed each opening and before long rattlers began showing from every direction, almost faster than Winston and I could catch them and drop them into an escape-proof box. We hunted there for four or five hours and caught a grand total of 99 rattlers. One reason we stayed so long is because we wanted to get one more for an even 100. Although that failed, I'm going to claim 99 as a record from one den until someone proves differently.

Unless you overdo it, you can hunt the same dens year after year. Should you clean out a den, however, it'll be three or four years before snakes return in any numbers. Winston and I went back to the "99" den, as I call it, a few years later and caught 53 more rattlers.

About 30 different species of rattlesnakes live in the United States. These include the prairie, sidewinder, canebrake, and timber rattlers, but the one we hunt is the biggest and most aggressive of all, the Western diamondback rattlesnake. The largest one I've caught was in northern Mexico. That snake was five feet eight inches long, but what was impressive was the bulk. It was about as big around as a medium-sized fence post. The snake with the most number of rattles I've caught had 16.

Snake hunting is not for the weak of heart or the careless.

It's extremely rare to find a snake with that many rattles. Some people believe a snake grows a new rattle every year and the number of rattles is an indication of age. Not true. Usually the snake gets another rattle every time it sheds its skin, about twice a year with adults, up to four times with young snakes. But as a snake gets older, it seldom keeps all it gets; wear, age and breakage account for the loss of rattles.

The entire rattle is a hornlike substance made up of segments that interlock. When the snake shakes its tail, each rattle strikes the adjacent one to create the familiar sound. And once you hear the sound, I guarantee you'll never forget it. No one seems to know what role the rattle is supposed to play. It's been proven that the rattle isn't used to warn prey, since this would make it more difficult to get food, nor is it a mating call or sound. But *I* know what it's for; it's a rattler's way of scaring hell out of someone like me.

To catch rattlesnakes, you've got to find some. As with any hunting, that's the obvious first step. And you've got to know where

A piece of copper tubing is used to squirt gas far back in the den.

to look, along the southwest side of a rocky hill, up high enough where the den entrance isn't subject to flooding. Dens don't have openings toward the north so they can keep out the fierce winter wind. If your timing is right, you likely will find a snake or two or three around a crevice or hole in the hillside. There're probably more inside.

Through most of the winter the snakes are in a dead stupor. Only when the weather begins to moderate do they commence stirring. On any bright and shirtsleeves day from late February on through March, the rattlers are likely to crawl into the open, coiling to take a siesta in the warm sunshine, then retreat back into the den during the cold night.

One way to hunt is simply to walk along and capture the ones out sunning. When I'm hunting the flat, rockless terrain of south Texas, where the snakes are not concentrated, I just drive the pasture roads and look for them. The ideal day is cloudy, high humidity, with a temperature in the 80s. Some of these south Texas rattlers grow into real jumbos. One is so heavy it leaves a telltale "drag" where it crosses a road. When I find one of these, I get out and follow the trail. More often than not I find the snake in the open and it's mine.

But raiding a den is more specialized. Sometimes you have to move rocks around and readjust the terrain just to get inside.

I remember a hunt that I took with Winston, J. D. Taylor, and Bernie Smith. We were hunting on a ranch south of Sweetwater where we'd never been before. One sunny shirtsleeves afternoon we scattered and scrounged the rimrocks for dens, looking for sunning snakes. We also used hand-held mirrors to reflect light into holes, hoping to see a snake or find slick areas indicating the serpents had been crawling in and out.

If you hunt snakes you learn that the entrance is not indicative of the den's size. Sometimes an opening not much larger than a fruit jar might lead to a labyrinth of underground tunnels and crevices.

As I eased along the slope, watching where I was stepping, I came upon two rattlesnakes of moderate size sunning themselves on a rocky ledge. I prodded the snakes with a long stick, and each one immediately whipped into a tight coil and began buzzing. I continued to agitate the snakes until they had enough and took off, quickly vanishing into a closeby crevice, returning to their den. I marked the spot with a white rag tied on a tree branch because sometimes it's difficult to find the precise place again.

Overnight, the March weather turned nasty. A cold front moved in, droppng the temperature to near freezing. With the sharp wind I imagine the chill factor was below zero. Thankfully the rock out-

I ease the catcher around its neck and—gotcha!

cropping where we were to gas served as an effective windbreak. Even so, I had to keep reminding myself how much fun I was having.

We'd driven as close as we could and packed the necessary equipment to the den entrance. We had a pressurized can, the pump-up type used to spray shrubs and gardens, a nozzle 10 feet in length improvised from copper tubing. Inside the can was gasoline. A smart aleck once asked me if I recommended regular or no-lead. He said he'd heard that no-lead created less pollution.

I do know that whatever the octane, the pressurized liquid is dangerous. You don't want someone smoking a cigarette while fooling around with the spray can.

We had to take shovels and crowbars and move some rocks before we could shove the copper-tubing nozzle far back into the den. Only a small amount of gas is sprayed; if you put in too much gas, the snakes might die before they can reach fresh air.

Every member of the party had either a hook or a catcher. The hook is nothing more than a long handle with a hook on the end, used to pull a snake into the open before it can dart back into the den. A catcher is improvised from electrical conduit about six feet long. A piece of plastic clothesline is doubled through the pipe, leaving a loop at one end, with the two loose ends tied to a piece of wood that serves as a handle. The loop is dropped over the rattler's head and pulled snug with a yank of the handle. The reptile then is deposited into some sort of escape-proof container.

For anyone other than the expert, grabbing a rattler with your hands is nothing more than a dangerous stunt. Snakes are slippery, and big ones are incredibly strong. Anyone foolish enough to handle a virulent snake with his hands is asking for trouble.

When a rattlesnake first emerges from its den, it's apt to be groggy from the gas fumes and won't put up much protest. Nonetheless, keep in mind that a rattler is potentially dangerous. This danger element is what attracts many people to the sport, the same sort of weird fascination that has prompted many anglers to start fishing for sharks. But it really isn't all that hazardous for the person who is cautious, respects the snake, and goes about his business with a bit of common sense—and this includes always looking where you step.

Gas fumes forced this one to go to fresh air.

A den can have several entrances and a snake might emerge from most anywhere. While Winston and I gassed this den, the other hunters spread out to watch crevices that might be escape routes.

It was the pragmatic thing to do because soon snakes began coming from every which direction. We caught most of them, but a few sensed danger and went back into the den, probably crawling

This rattler is still groggy from the gas fumes.

into places where the gas fumes didn't reach. In a large, spread-out den, you seldom get total gas distribution.

I've never felt threatened by a rattler while snake hunting, pri-marily because I'm super cautious. Like on this hunt. One time I'd caught a struggling rattler and was turning to drop it into a deep wooden box, when right behind me another snake came slithering

by. I dropped the one I had into the box, then picked up this snake—
two for the price of one. And when it was over, we had 44 snakes
to show for our efforts.

A snake coming out of hibernation isn't going to be very alert or
aggressive, and this is particularly true of one under the influence
of gas. The snake has to "warm up" in the sun or shake off the
effects of a gas hangover before it will even rattle. I've seen some
sunning in late winter that I believe you could have picked up gently
without disturbing them. Or not so gently, as Russell Tinsley found
out.

We were hunting on Max Wenmohs' ranch near my home in
central Texas. I took Russell to a den I knew about and, sure
enough, we found two fairly large rattlers coiled beside the hole.
Russell said he wanted to take some pictures of the snakes before
I caught them and he eased around into position. But we had overlooked another rattler coiled in some grass on the other side of the
den entrance. As Russell circled, he put a foot down on the sleeping
snake. I don't know what the standing broad-jump record might
be, but I believe he broke it.

And the snake? It didn't move until I picked it up and dropped
it into a burlap bag.

Chapter 19

Tracking, Cheating, and Other Tricks

Some years ago an editor of a popular gun magazine came to Texas to hunt with me. I picked him up at the San Antonio Airport, and we drove more than 150 miles to a ranch near Laredo. Before we ever stuffed any cartridges into our rifles, I already had a suspicion that my guest wasn't a very good hunter.

He wasn't.

You no doubt wonder how I could pass judgment without seeing the man in action. Easy. In south Texas we were driving through country that was unfamiliar to the man. In fact, this terrain is unlike anyplace else. Yet the man showed no interest in the environment. He didn't ask any questions about the plant life or wildlife. Show me a person who's observant and curious about things and I'll show you someone who'll make a good hunter. When you're in the woods you have to be alert to what's going on.

If you start looking, you'll begin to see things you've never seen before. And the more you see, the more you'll want to see. There are a lot of clues laying around that tell a story.

One time Winston and I were in south Texas to hunt javelina with bows and arrows. There are a lot of javelina in this region, but there's also a lot of country for them to get lost in.

Bearded me tracked this Alaskan wolvervine several miles.

By being observant, Winston hit the jackpot the first morning out. We separated to prowl the *senderos*, as south Texas natives call roads and openings cut through the thornbrush. An overnight rain shower not only left the ground muddy, it wiped out all the wildlife sign.

So when Winston found javelina tracks crossing a *sendero*, he knew they were fresh. The wind was quartering, which was to his advantage. Javelina have poor eyesight but an acute sense of smell. Quietly and deliberately, Winston followed the tracks until, just ahead, he could hear the grunts of the javelina. Bent low, he slipped closer and saw five or six of the squat little animals tearing at prickly pear cactus, their favorite food. One of the javelina, an old boar, was bigger than the others. Winston got him with an arrow right behind the shoulder.

In Alaska, Dick Hemmen and I sighted a large wolverine from his airplane. The dark shape of the animal was easy to see as it loped across the snow field. We landed and picked up the wolverine's track. We trailed it for probably three miles until I had a chance for a shot and got my first wolverine.

While these incidents were different, they were alike in that successful tracking was the key to success. Tracks will tell you what animals are in an area, a good idea about their numbers, and, in some instances, even lead you to wildlife. But you have to know how to "read" the sign. That takes study and experience.

Tracks also can be beneficial in another way, when trailing a crippled animal. They will give you a direction to follow, a route where you can look for other clues such as blood, and, at times, even can tell you where the animal is hit and perhaps how badly it is wounded.

I remember one example. I was hunting with what I call a dude. When someone like this gets in the woods, he seems to let his mind go blank. This fellow had an easy shot at a whopper of a buck, the animal standing broadside about 100 yards away. I watched the whole thing. The man took a rest and fired and the deer ran off.

The hunter shook his head dejectedly. "I don't know how, but I aimed right behind the shoulder and I flat missed him," he said.

"Are you sure?" I asked.

"Damn right, didn't you see him run off?"

I knew better. The bullet had hit the deer, but I didn't know where. By carefully examining the scene, the exact place where the buck had been standing, I hoped to find out.

It didn't take me long to find tracks, then some hair and pieces of bone and blood. My companion was amazed; he said he had no idea the deer had been hit.

After trailing the buck a short way, I came to where I could see the tracks plainly. One hind hoof was digging in deeper than the tracks of the forefeet, while the other hind hoof was making a scraping drag. By that I could determine he was hit in the right hind leg. Blood on the bushes showed how high the wound was; he was hit just above the hock. Fortunately, the deer was bleeding profusely. I soon came to where he had lain down briefly and left a huge puddle of blood.

Rather than sticking to the trail, I returned to the pickup and drove to the rancher's house. He had some trained dogs, which are legal in Texas for trailing crippled deer. We put the dogs on the trail and within minutes they had the weakened buck at bay. Because I had the knowledge to figure out where the buck was hit and how badly, I was able to save a trophy, make a hunter happy, and keep the hunter from being run off the place. This rancher doesn't look kindly on a hunter who will shoot at a deer and not make any effort to go and look to see if he hit the animal or not.

Never *assume* you missed. Always check. I've seen deer shot through their hearts that dashed off, but they went only a short distance before dropping.

Before leaving the spot where you were standing when you fired, pick out some familiar landmark that will direct you to where the deer was at the same time. It might be a stump or a rock or a tree or anything. Look at the landmark closely so you can identify it when you get there.

Easy identification would seem obvious, but not always. I once shot a buck on the other side of a deep canyon in Colorado. The range straight across wasn't all that far, but it was a long walk—down and then up—to get to the deer. Before moving, Winston and I picked out a dead tree that would show us exactly where the buck lay.

The trouble was, when we got to the opposite side, dead trees were everywhere and they all looked the same. We knew the deer was nearby, but we didn't know where. We began a systematic search and more than an hour later found the buck.

If you shoot at a deer or some other big-game animal and it rears up and falls backward, that usually indicates a chest or heart hit.

One trick I sometimes use when night calling is to rest my rifle on my camera tripod.

But some wounded deer take off as though they haven't been touched.

Find precisely where the buck was standing by looking for tracks. There might not be any blood, at least not right there, since some deer shot with high-velocity rifles bleed internally rather than externally because of the absence of exit holes. I've seen some deer go several hundred yards before leaving steady trails of blood.

While there might not be blood, there will be hair if the buck was hit. In many instances the type of hair will tell you where the bullet struck. With a whitetail deer, for instance, long white hair indicates a belly or flank hit; dark hair comes from the chest, shoulder or lower part of the neck.

If the blood is foamy, you know your bullet hit the lungs. And sometimes you can get close to the ground and smell where the animal was hit. If the bullet got the paunch area and damaged intestines, there will be a very definite fermented, soured smell.

Trailing a wounded animal takes patience. Use tissue paper or maybe even sticks and rocks to mark the trail as you go along. If you lose the trail you might have to backtrack. And don't walk in the trail the animal made. Leave it undisturbed.

Dad was the best at trailing of anyone I have known. I learned by watching him. While on a trail he would spend most of the time crawling on his knees. He had good eyesight and woodsmanship. He could find tracks and blood drops when no one else could see them. I've watched him trail when there was nothing more than a speck of blood every few feet. One time he spent an entire day trailing a wounded buck deer. He'd occasionally lose the trail, but he wouldn't give up. He'd backtrack and start unraveling the mystery again. Finally, he trailed the deer to the edge of a pool on

Since older bucks would hide in the bordering brush until darkness told them it was safe to enter a field, I learned how to cheat on them.

Double Horn Creek, near where I now live. The weakened animal had probably drowned; he was lying at the bottom of the pool with only one antler showing near the surface.

One of the most valuable lessons Dad taught me was to never give up on a deer, not as long as there was a chance. He never quit until he lost the trail completely, or he was able to tell where the animal was hit and he knew he would never get it. I saw him find many deer that I was ready to give up for lost.

He also taught me about cheating, Nah, it isn't anything illegal. This is a technique where I cheat on a deer or some other animal.

It helped me get the trophy Colorado black bear mentioned earlier. From tracks, I could tell which trail the bear was using when he visited the bait. But since the size of the track showed him to be a big bear, this indicated age, which also indicated wisdom. The sly old customer probably would not come to the bait until total darkness.

So I cheated to gain a few minutes of precious light. I moved up the trail about 100 yards to watch. The idea was to ambush the bear traveling toward the bait rather than waiting right at the bait. And it paid off.

The same ploy produced numerous times while hunting deer near

I made a whimpering noise with my lips and this coyote barked at me.

my central Texas home. Deer here, like in many parts of the country, steal into agricultural fields to feed, but the old bucks usually won't enter a field until after dark. I remember a wildlife biologist telling me about taking a census of deer in Nebraska; he would spotlight fields at night and count the animals.

The sharper bucks, I found, would come in late afternoon to the bordering brush along my family's oat field and would hide there until nightfall when they felt secure enough to go in and eat. So I'd scout until I found a well-traveled trail deer were following to the field, then I'd slip up this main trail to where it broke into several smaller feeder trails. That's where I'd hide.

The one thing a human has over a wild animal is intelligence. He has to figure ways to outslick a crafty animal like the whitetail. It isn't easy because nature has blessed most wildlife with a formidable defense.

Man has been going to war with coyotes for years, for example, and in most cases the coyotes are winning. They are adaptable and smart, a hard combination to beat.

One way to outtrick a coyote is to put someone 50 yards or so downwind from the caller, depending on the terrain. He should be in a position where he can see farther downwind than he can in any other direction. More times than not, the wily coyote is going to circle downwind, to test the scent to find out what's going on. The person posted downwind can sometimes get a shot before the coyote realizes what's going on.

This trickery will work on other wild animals, too. Just like in a football game, it's a matter of devising an offense that is better than the defense. When in the woods, be observant, curious, and always thinking. That's the way to win.

Chapter 20

Guns and Loads

In my years of hunting I've tried about every caliber there is and, through a process of elimination, I've settled on the guns that do the best job for me. I tend to overgun rather than undergun; when I shoot at something I want it dead on the spot.

One thing I've learned, however, is that bullet placement is the most important consideration of all. I'm not what you'd call a lead slinger; I don't just shoot and hope. I'm pretty selective about my shots.

If the animal is broadside, I've gotten into the habit of aiming behind the shoulder, about halfway up. This lung shot is a quick and humane killer, it doesn't ruin as much hide as some other shots do, and it doesn't destroy much edible meat. It also gives you more margin of error than anyplace else you aim. If your bullet is slightly low, you'll get the heart region; slightly higher and you'll break the spine.

But no matter what game animal you're hunting, it's imperative that you be familiar with your gun, knowing where it shoots at various ranges. You should be able to aim and fire without thinking of any of the mechanical procedures.

I'm also a fanatic about safety. I never point my gun at anything I don't intend to shoot. I've had hunters look at me through their rifle scopes. That's frightening. I've also been with hunters who are much too casual with their firearms. They swing the muzzles around or prop loaded rifles or shotguns against something where, if a gun tipped over, it might go off. I never carry a cocked gun or one with the safety off. I don't activate the gun to fire position until I'm ready to shoot.

You also won't get me into an argument about one caliber versus another. I'm not much on ballistics. To me, a gun is a tool that, when it goes bang, something drops. The right gun for me might not be the right gun for you, certainly not in the type of action you choose. Pick the action—bolt, pump, autoloading or lever—that makes you feel most comfortable.

I'm also not much on handloading; I use mostly factory loads. Whenever I need a special cartridge, I depend on my friend Leonard Storey. Leonard is a self-professed "gun nut" who has the uncanny ability to match a certain load with a certain rifle, without much experimentation. Each rifle, he says, has a different personality, and a handloaded cartridge can be matched to any rifle to give optimum performance. So he does the home brewing and I do the field testing.

I'm a staunch believer in patterning a shotgun. I want to know how the gun handles differently sized shot at different ranges. You can't know too much about your gun. It might be the slight edge between bragging and crying about the one that got away.

Things have been written about guns that simply aren't true. I've heard that a bullet traveling at high velocity will explode if it strikes a branch or bush. Baloney! It might deflect, but it won't actually explode.

If an animal is standing directly behind brush, I've never hesitated to shoot through the brush—and I've had good success. I've shot at four or five deer, maybe more, standing in the brush, in places where other, more cautious hunters probably wouldn't even have taken the chance, and I've gotten every one. One time years ago, I shot at a deer with a .30-30 and the bullet passed through a dead cedar limb as big as your wrist, yet it still retained enough speed and penetration to kill the deer. If you know anything about cedar (juniper), after a tree dies and dries, the wood is almost as hard as concrete.

For coyote hunting I like either the .243 Winchester or 6mm Remington.

When discussing the guns I use for various game, I want you to understand these are not the only ones that will do the job. There are a whole bunch of calibers, for example, that will work on white-tail deer. I'm only going to tell you what I use, what works best for me.

Fox. There is a lot of air around a diminutive fox and the critter is jittery, never standing still for long. You might have best success with a shotgun. A full-choke 12 gauge with No. 4 or 6 shot is the ticket. The size of shot isn't all that important; use the shot that your shotgun patterns best. A shotgun kills by pattern density rather than individual shot. Aim at the head; a fox isn't that difficult to kill.

I use a rifle because it's more of a challenge and varmint hunting is good practice. One reason that I'm a pretty country-fair shot on big game is because I shoot a lot at live targets, and shooting is like anything, the more you practice the better you get.

The .22 rimfire is not potent enough for foxes. You'll often cripple rather than kill cleanly. The .22 Hornet or the .222 Remington is a good caliber. I use what Leonard Storey calls "Murry's varmint load." It's a toned-down .222, 14 grains of 4227 powder and a 45-grain Sierra bullet. This load delivers about 1,900 feet per second. It's real deadly. Leonard and I tried five different loads before we settled on this one.

Coyote. The coyote is a tough hombre. The .222 Remington is a little light. I've seen coyotes shot behind the shoulder with the .222 that got up and ran away, some that were never found. One time Winston and I were hunting with Willie Esse, Jr., in south Texas and a big male coyote was gut shot with a .222. The bullet knocked him down, but he got up running. As he dashed across a clearing, his intestines were trailing from the huge bullet-exit hole and, without breaking stride, he whipped his head around and bit off his innards. He didn't run very far, but that gives some hint about how tough coyotes are.

For coyotes, I've found either the .243 Winchester or the 6mm Remington to be about ideal. There's no reason to recommend one over the other; they are almost identical in performance.

Bobcat. The .243 or the 6mm is most deadly for bobcats, but either will cause considerable damage to the hide with most hits. If you want a bobcat pelt to sell or maybe to make into a tapestry or rug, you don't want the hide to have a large hole where the bullet came out. To keep damage to the hide at a minimum, I use the loaded-down .222 (the same as for foxes) and I've had good success with it, although of course with this load there's more of a premium on precise accuracy.

Raccoon. The .22 WRF Magnum is adequate for hunting raccoons. Also good is the loaded-down .222. For factory loads, I like either the .22 Hornet or the .222. With a shotgun, use the same combination that you'd use for fox.

Squirrel. I like the .22 rimfire with Long Rifle cartridges for hunting squirrels. The .22 Short is a plinking cartridge, not a hunting load. There's really no reason to recommend the .22 Long, it being a hybrid, the powder charge of the Long Rifle, a Short bullet. I doubt that most places even stock Longs anymore.

I got this Colorado buck with my favorite mule deer cartridge, the 7mm Magnum.

I always aim for the head for two reasons, either I hit—with no edible meat damaged—or I miss cleanly.

For a shotgun, I use a full-choke 12-gauge, No. 6 shot, because my gun patterns this shot very well, a tight pattern with good distribution of shot out to about 40 yards. But No. 7½ shot will do if your gun patterns this size better. It doesn't take much to stop a squirrel.

Wild Turkey. Use No. 4 or 6 shot, whichever patterns best in a full-choke 12-gauge, for wild turkeys. A magnum load is a little more insurance. Aim for the neck and head.

I also hunt with a rifle, both spring and fall. Some people have tried to suggest that a rifle is unsporting. A turkey is just as dead whether it is hit with a load of shotgun pellets or a bullet. I can't see how it really makes any difference. My pet caliber is that loaded-down .222. It's a real killer, but it doesn't tear up much meat. I've shot turkeys in the rear and in the chest without doing a whole lot of damage. But your best shot is a little high, above the breast, about where the wing attaches to the body, although at times it's difficult to determine exactly where this is. In a factory load, the .22 Hornet is a good turkey gun.

Crow. Any shotgun, modified or improved-cylinder choke, will do the job on crows. No. 7½ or 8 shot is adequate. I sometimes hunt with a .410 for the challenge. When you hunt crows or magpies, use the same shotgun and load you use for doves and quail. Crow shooting is good practice. And if you reload your own shells, you can do about twice the shooting for the same money you pay for factory shells.

Whitetail Deer. I've used many different calibers for whitetails. For all-purpose use, the old dependable .30-06, .308, and .270 are hard to beat.

If I'm not hunting a trophy, only a deer to eat, I'll use the .243 with its 100-grain bullet and aim for the head or neck. For a trophy, I'll use the biggest deer gun I own, a 7mm Magnum. In trophy hunting I usually get only one chance and I want to make it count. This way I can take whatever shot I get, broadside or head on or running straight away. A bullet in the rear end is one of the most deadly of shots. When I'm hunting a trophy, I don't worry that much about any meat I lose.

The type of gun you select depends a great deal on where you're hunting. If your chances will be close, less than 100 yards in dense woods, the dependable .30-30 is adequate. In some places you legally can use only shotguns and rifled slugs, which are deadly. In more

I used a Model 600 Remington .308 to get this Alaskan caribou.

open country, where a shot can vary from close to more than 200 yards, you'll need a flatter-shooting rifle.

But again, choosing the caliber and type of action you like is only a beginning. You've got to become familiar with the rifle and know how it performs, where the bullet impacts from 25 to 200 or maybe 300 yards. For many years I hunted with a Remington Model 760 pump action, .30-06 caliber. That gun and I were the best of friends and together we got many deer. The bullet would be about an inch high at 100 yards, yet it dropped a full 15 inches at 300. I knew exactly where to aim at any intermediate range and I seldom missed.

But one more bit of advice: you'll be better off settling on one type action and one caliber. You might even use this gun for varmint hunting. The more you use it, the more familiar with it you'll become. You won't have to search for the safety. The entire shooting process will become almost subconscious.

Mule Deer. Mule deer live in country where a typical shot might be at long range. You need a caliber that not only kills, but reaches a long way with a flat trajectory. I've been using the 7mm Magnum for years and I've had great success with it.

Elk. I also use the 7mm Magnum for elk, but bullet placement has to be exact. Elk are big, tough, and thick through the body. You need lots of bullet penetration to pass through the animal. Another caliber I can recommend is the .300 H&H Magnum, which will drop a large bull elk in his tracks. It's also a good all-purpose cartridge for mule deer, moose, and other big game.

Black Bear. The .30-06 or .308 is hard to beat for black bear. A black bear is not all that hard to kill, but you need accurate bullet placement. Hit the animal behind the shoulder, about midway up, and you've got a dead bear. If you hunt over a bait, most shots will

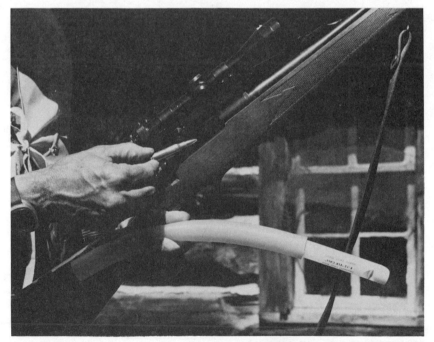

For elk hunting, I recommend a powerful load like the .300 H & H Magnum.

be at close range. Again, it's important to know how your gun per-forms because at close range, as the bullet goes up in its natural trajectory, there's a tendency to overshoot.

While you're getting familiar with your rifle, shoot at least twice, preferably three times at each intermediate range. Even with a good, solid rest there's margin for human error. The grouping of the three bullet holes will tell you how your rifle performs at that range.

For night calling, you need some sort of shooting light on your rifle.

You're going to burn quite a bit of ammunition in this process, but it's worth it. And, as a footnote, don't forget to check your rifle's accuracy before you go hunting, especially if it's been some time since you fired the gun. I've seen many a deer missed because a hunter "assumed" his rifle was on target when in fact it wasn't. A scope sight mounted properly can take a good deal of punishment, but sometimes only a slight jolt can rearrange the alignment. It's better to be sure than sorry.

Patterning a shotgun is even simpler. While this tells you how tight and dense the pattern is at various ranges, it also tells you where the main part of the pattern is going to be. On some shotguns it might be slightly high to the right, or slightly low to the left. It's important to know where the shot is going when you pull down on live game.

Obtain several pieces of paper more than 30 inches square. Newsprint from a local newspaper is good. Tape two sheets together. Get a refrigerator carton or a comparable large chunk of cardboard so you can staple the paper to it for support. The only other thing you need is a 15-inch piece of string tied to a pencil or ballpoint pen.

Stand the cardboard-supported paper and step off 40 yards. Aim directly at the center and fire. Now take the 15-inch radius of string, find the center and the most dense part of the pattern, and, holding the end of the string at the center, use the pencil or pen to draw a 30-inch circle. Study the pattern to see if you're getting most of the shot in the circle and an even distribution rather than scattered dense patches. A full-choke pattern will, of course, be tighter than modified or improved cylinder. Again, one shot is inconclusive. Fire three or four times to determine if the patterns you get are consistent.

Now place the paper at 35 yards and fire two or three shots and study the pattern. Repeat this at 30, 25, and finally 20 yards. You'll get an immediate picture of your pattern at these various ranges, and you'll better understand how your gun performs. And you'll be a better hunter. As I've stressed, the better prepared and organized you are, the better your odds for success.

Chapter 21

Bowhunting

I think every gun hunter should also hunt with a bow. He'll learn more from bowhunting than he ever thought possible.

Since you have to have your quarry close (the closer the better), you do your homework a bit more efficiently. You become more thorough and organized—scouting and learning animal behavior—and more patient. A long-shooting firearm is sometimes a crutch; you depend on it to cover your mistakes and it doesn't.

Becoming what Fred Bear calls a "two-season hunter" makes good sense. You can take advantage of the early archery seasons. Even if you don't score with your bow, you'll be preparing for the gun season. You can't learn anything about animals unless you get in the woods with them and mix it up. Reading about a subject is a start, but there's a long way to go. I'm reminded of the story about the person with a little knowledge: he knows just enough about the subject to be dangerous.

To shoot something with a bow and arrow, you must know how to use it. I've done some competitive shooting with a bow and I've also played some golf and the two sports are similar; it takes time and practice to master the fundamentals to the point where you have reasonable accuracy. You don't become proficient at either overnight.

I won't profess to recommend what equipment or so-called "tackle" to buy. If there's a pro shop in your town, that's the place to

Many archers prefer the compound bow with its cables, wheels, and pulleys.

go. Otherwise, find someone who is into bowhunting and ask his advice. Let him show you the different types of bows. You might feel more comfortable with a compound bow—a contraption with wheels, pulleys, and cables—or maybe you'll prefer the clean lines of a recurve bow. Properly weighted arrows have to be matched to the bow for accuracy. Buying equipment and learning to use it doesn't make you a bowhunter, but it's a step in the normal progression. You've got the entire off-season to learn to shoot the bow proficiently. That means practice, hours of practice. If you can consistently group three or four arrows in a six-inch circle at twenty-five yards, you can kill a deer. I've found that the person who regularly makes the top scores on an archery range is more interested in the shooting than the hunting.

I do believe that a hunting bow should have a minimum of 45 pounds pull. Buy the strongest bow *you can handle*. Being able to pull a 60-pound bow to full draw doesn't mean you can handle the bow. If you tend to shake and quiver at full draw, you're only handicapping your chances. No one can tell you how much draw-poundage you can handle. That's up to you.

Many bowhunters begin at one draw weight and slowly work up. With the right exercise program, the muscles you use to draw a bow get stronger. Ask the manager of the archery pro shop how you can increase your draw strength.

Most people who get into bowhunting start with deer, then maybe go to something else, but Winston and I started with something else and went to deer. The reason we took up bowhunting was to shoot raccoons after we'd called them close. We took pictures of the sequence, thinking this would make an unusual angle for a magazine article. From that point, we became intrigued with the challenge of bowhunting. We had relatively quick success with the bow on deer because we knew what we were doing. 'Coon hunting taught us a lot.

I've always preached that you can learn more about hunting by hunting than you can on the target range. Field conditions are entirely different. You have to anticipate situations and adapt to them. I know I learned more about bowhunting while hunting cottontails or jackrabbits than I ever could have shooting at paper targets.

And believe me, to bushwack a skitterish whitetail deer, you have to know what you're doing. You've got to be like a squirrel; you've got to get up in a tree. There's just no way you can maneuver around on the ground without the deer seeing you nine times out of 10. Above the deer's line of normal sight, you can move a bit more and get away with it, but as I've stressed many times previously, your movements must be controlled. Learn what you can

I prefer a quiver that attaches to the bow.

do, and when the time's right do it. A bowhunter has to use the element of surprise to his utmost advantage.

One thing you're going to find right off is that shooting from a tree is different from shooting on the ground. Many times you'll be drawing the bow from awkward angles. Practice shooting from a tree. Around each of my stands I like to measure the distance to landmarks so I always know precisely how far away a deer is. My bowhunting philosophy is to have the deer close, real close. There's less margin for human error. I guess that's why I've had success. Seldom have I missed or crippled a deer with a shot.

Another thing you should do is get your tree stand ready long before the season. Give the deer time to become accustomed to its presence. Clear out any branches that might be in your way and build some sort of platform to sit on, if this is permitted where you hunt. I've spent many an hour sitting on an uncomfortable branch. When building my stand I like to disturb the scenery as little as possible. Don't put anything into the tree that doesn't need to be there. Whitetails are just naturally suspicious. Once they locate your stand, they never forget it.

One time I shot at a young buck and missed, only nipping the top of his back just enough to cut the skin. When the spot healed it covered with white hair, a telltale mark that was almost like a brand. I knew that deer and he knew the location of my stand. Everytime he passed through the area he got nervous, stopping to stomp his foot, a signal that ran every deer within hearing distance away.

But I outfoxed that buck. I moved into another tree a few yards away. I didn't disturb anything; I didn't even snap off a twig. I straddled a large limb no more than 10 feet off the ground and waited. The deer were so preoccupied with the original stand that they ignored me in the nearby tree. Another point worth repeating is that you've got to keep the deer guessing.

Successful bowhunting takes time, lots of quiet waiting. I'm convinced that trying to sneak up on a whitetail without it knowing you're there is a losing cause. You can stalk mule deer, however. Most reside where you can see them in the distance, so you can plan your sneak attack to take advantage of the wind and any available cover. The type of terrain will dictate your hunting strategy. But as I've said, under most circumstances, I believe in ambush hunting or trail watching. I'm convinced this is your best chance.

Whether I am hunting with a gun or bow, I'm a stickler for detail. I want everything right. When I started out in archery, I was an instinctive shooter; that is, I sort of "looked" the arrow to the target. Later on, I tried a sight and, sure enough, it improved my accuracy. But it wasn't the same. Some of the challenge was gone, so I gave

For deer hunting, I like to make like a squirrel and climb a tree.

up the sight. This is the sort of thing you must decide for yourself.

Yet, one thing you should decide to use is a sharp broadhead. Never compromise. A bullet kills primarily by shock, an arrow by hemorrhage. And you need a sharp broadhead to induce profuse bleeding. It's like you cut yourself with a sharp knife; there isn't much pain but lots of blood. With a dull edge, there is considerable pain but not much blood.

I shot a buck once that was feeding near my tree stand. I thought I'd hit him but I couldn't be sure. The arrow hit the ground on the opposite side of the animal but he didn't even jump or flinch. He kept on feeding. In about a minute or so, he toppled over dead. I'd shot him through the heart. The deer never knew he'd been hit.

Many people believe a broadhead is sharp when it isn't. The edge has to be sharp enough to shave. Some broadheads have replaceable razor-blade inserts; when one gets dull, you pop it out and put in another.

Yet, no matter how sharp the broadhead, you've got to have accurate arrow placement. A common mistake is to aim at the entire deer rather than at a specific spot. Aim behind the shoulder about halfway up. If you put a sharp broadhead there, you've got a dead deer.

For several years, I was really gung-ho about bowhunting. I killed 13 deer. Then, instead of merely deer hunting, I began trophy hunting. From that, I went on to wildlife photography, which is similar to bowhunting but even more demanding (see the next chapter). I'm always looking for different things to do, different challenges.

One challenge was trying to shoot a coyote with an arrow. I've sent arrows in the direction of a bunch of them. It isn't uncommon for a coyote to see an arrow coming and dodge at the last possible instant. Winston and I killed a few coyotes along the way, but, based on the number we actually shot at, our batting average wasn't much to brag about. If a major-league baseball player had the same average, he'd earn a quick trip back to the minors.

One thing for sure, when hunting with a predator call and a bow, there aren't many dull moments. You get some fast action.

The two sports—calling and bowhunting—go together nicely. You need to have an animal real close to shoot it with a bow and arrow, and the intent of calling is to bring a critter close.

Hunting as a team also offers advantages. I've done the calling for many archers. The idea is to separate the caller and shooter by several yards. The animal homes in on the sound, and the archer has more freedom of movement. The most crucial time in bowhunting is when the bow is drawn. There's no way to eliminate the movement, so it must be timed perfectly. Wait until the critter's

I like aluminum arrows with interchangeable heads.

head is turned or is behind a bush before making your play. If you have eye contact with the animal, don't move a hair.

If you stay with it long enough, every once in awhile you'll hit the jackpot. Like the New Jersey hunter I guided. I've forgotten his name, but that was the first and last time I've ever accepted money to guide someone. I don't have the time for that sort of thing.

Anyway, we were hunting at night in the south Texas brush country. I'd scouted the locale and knew where to go. We walked quietly to our hunting site, me leading the way with the headlight beam on my feet instead of flashing around. When we were ready to call, I adjusted the light and swept it around us for a quick look before I commenced to call. I spotted eyes not more than 40 or 50

Bowhunting and calling are sports made for each other.

yards away. I only had to lip squeak a few times and a bobcat came within 15 yards. The archer shot it.

The next stop took a little longer—about 20 minutes—before another of the stubby-tailed cats showed. The New Jersey hunter also got this one. Imagine, two bobcats in one night. A bowhunter is fortunate if he kills one during his entire hunting career, or at least one that's been called. You might get one that's been bayed by hounds, but I never thought that to be sporting. If the bobcat is a sitting duck, it doesn't make any difference what you shoot it with.

We all realize that the bow can be a handicap, especially when an animal stays out a few yards beyond effective shooting range. This is what makes the sport both frustrating and fascinating. But how about the handicap of having an animal too close? That's what happened to Lynn Willis.

You probably remember me telling about Lynn in previous chapters, how a fox got in a tree with him, how he wrestled a mule deer in Colorado. Lynn has this knack of getting into predicaments.

We were hunting together, me doing the calling, Lynn the shooting. Separated a couple dozen yards. I couldn't see him nor could he see me in the thick thornbrush.

Consequently, Lynn saw the coyote coming, but I didn't. The coyote was trailing him, following the same path he had walked. Why, I don't know. We weren't using any type of scent that might have attracted him.

Head down, the coyote trotted toward where Lynn was hidden. Lynn raised his bow, drew the arrow, and waited for the animal to get close. He thought the animal surely would stop. But instead, the critter ran right to his feet, so close that when Lynn released the arrow, it never left the string. The broadhead struck a tooth and glanced off, cutting the coyote's mouth. We trailed him a ways before the blood trail stopped. Obviously we didn't hurt that coyote.

But Lynn did have a story to pass on to his grandkids—if they believe him. I was there, and I still find it hard to believe.

Chapter 22

Camera Hunting

Hunting with a camera is fun and one heck of a challenge. The difference between it and gun hunting is about the same as the difference between driving an automobile and piloting a jet airplane. I think you can learn more in a year of serious camera hunting than you can in a lifetime of hunting with a gun. And I can think of no better "trophy" than a quality enlargement of some game animal you've captured on film.

There's one advantage of camera hunting that you might not have thought of: you can "hunt" in places where firearms and even bows and arrows are prohibited—wildlife refuges, state and national parks, and some wildlife management areas. Many landowners also will welcome the camera hunter but not the gun hunter.

I can understand why most hunters want to shoot something; they don't get that many chances. But you can do both, camera hunting and gun or bowhunting. In most states you can legally take fur-bearing animals only during the winter season, when pelts can be sold. But there's nothing to keep you from calling wildlife at other times of the year and taking pictures. You even have your choice of a mouth-blown call or an electronic caller. Few restrictions are placed on the camera hunter.

Like the hunt Ed Kozicky and I took in June in Custer State Park in South Dakota's Black Hills. Ed was then conservation director of Olin Corporation's Nilo Farms and he's a game-calling buff. We made several stops through the park and called many deer, plus a couple coyotes. Not many came close enough for any decent pictures, but that's part of it. You have to work at it and be patient to get good wildlife photos.

When taking photos, I usually go afield alone. There's less chance of being detected. I use an electronic caller most times, because it leaves both hands free for manipulating the camera. Also, I can situate the auxiliary speaker away from me so the animal is attracted to it and I have a better chance of snapping a picture without spooking the critter.

Thanks to automatic cameras, the technical aspects of photography have been much simplified. In most instances I will use a Nikon camera and a Nikkor 50- to 300mm zoom lens, but many cameras on the market will do a satisfactory job. There's no reason to wreck the family budget to get into wildlife photography; a medium-priced camera will do just as well as the most expensive models. Top-of-the-line cameras are for the professional who uses his most every day.

The lens—not the camera—determines sharpness and quality. Some independent companies produce lenses with brand names like Sigma, Vivitar, Tamron, Tokina, and Soligor that give excellent results at a price cheaper than comparable lenses offered by the better-known camera manufacturers.

For wildlife photography, it's imperative you get a 35mm camera with interchangeable lenses. These cameras come with 50mm lenses, which are fine for general snapshot photography, or you may have the option of purchasing only the camera body and a telephoto lens to fit it. One feature you should have is a battery-powered film advance. This way you can advance the film by merely pressing a button; you can keep your subject in focus and never have to lower the camera from your eye.

We're not going to deal with camera equipment here because development is ongoing and somebody dreams up a new feature almost every month. Go to a reputable photo store and let the salesman show you the various models and explain the advantages and disadvantages of each. Tell the salesperson that you intend to use your camera for wildlife photography.

Through the years, the 300mm lens has been my standby, although it really lacks sufficient magnification. A 50mm lens is considered normal, or what the human eye sees; thus, a 300 magnifies six times. But even with this, you have to have your subject at extremely close range. Fifty yards away is too far. A 400mm lens is better if you can hold it steady enough to get sharp results. I never use a tripod because I need some freedom of movement. A wild animal seldom stays where you want it to stay. You've got to follow it—and that's hard to do with a tripod. Any lens more powerful than a 400mm is impractical the way I shoot. I simply have to depend on getting my subject closer, one way or another.

But the faster shutter speed you can utilize, the better your chances of "freezing" your subject for sharpness. That's why, for the beginner, I recommend a fast film: Tri-X for black and white, Ektachrome 400 for slides, Kodacolor 400 for color prints. If your camera is capable of a shutter speed of 1/1000th of a second and available light lets you employ that setting, so much to your ad-

I'm always looking for the unusual photo, like this gobbling turkey.

vantage. Otherwise, with a film of slower ASA rating and thus a slower shutter speed, you might get slightly blurry photos because it's difficult to hold a telephoto lens steady, particularly in the excitement of photographing wild animals and birds. (If some sort of rest—such as a tree—is handy, brace the lens against it to minimize camera shake.)

With an automatic camera, either the aperture (f stop) or the shutter speed is adjusted automatically to the light. In some models it's a combination of both. But a good rule of thumb to remember is the higher the ASA number of the film, the faster the shutter speed for sharper photographs. Although higher speed films show more grain, the quality isn't all that bad.

The most common mistake of the camera hunter is to snap away when the subject is out of range. You might think the subject is plenty close, but when you get your prints or slides back, you can barely find it. My first futile attempt was with a Kodak Brownie 620 camera. I called a gray fox within 10 feet and took its picture. I was real proud of myself until I got the print back. I had to look hard to even find it, not much more than a speck.

When looking through your camera's viewfinder, the subject should fill at least half of it, preferably more. To give some inkling as to what this involves, find an object at home about the same size as a fox. Then, looking through your camera, walk toward the object until it almost fills the viewfinder. Now lower the camera and see how close you are. Even with a 400mm telephoto lens, I think you'll be amazed at how close the subject must be. That's what makes wildlife photography so challenging.

One thing to keep in mind is that the camera's a tool, nothing more. It records only what you see at the instant you press the shutter release. Practice with it at home until you can operate it without a lot of involved thinking.

Focusing is a persistent problem. With a telephoto lens, there isn't much depth of field, so there's little leeway for error. When I get ready to call, the last thing I do is to measure the distance to every nearby landmark, using the camera lens to get the object sharp, then noting the distance on the footage scale of the lens. This way, if something comes in, I know how far away it is by its relationship to a landmark, and I can set the lens at that distance and snap a picture. This saves a little bit of time, which is critical in wildlife photography. Some cameras have automatic features that help. You can get one, for example, with a shutter that trips the instant the subject comes into focus at a preselected range. In choosing a camera model, you have to weigh a number of factors— size, weight, reliability, lenses, speed of operation, special features, and so on.

When taking pictures at a wildlife refuge, where the animals and birds are somewhat tame, you might have the luxury of time to make all the necessary adjustments and shoot at your convenience. In fact, I would recommend you begin by shooting pictures where you have some control over your subjects. It gives you some idea as to what the "sport" is all about.

Not only are many of these subjects somewhat tame, however, they look tame. They lack the awareness that makes the difference between an excellent and a ho-hum photo. To make your subject more alert, hold a short-range predator call between your lips.

It takes practice to capture a speedy coyote in midair like this.

Just before you snap the picture, blow on the call. The subject will perk up, with an alert look, and you'll have a much better photo.

When calling wild animals to the camera, things can happen so fast that you really don't have time to do everything right. My bugaboo is focusing on something coming directly at me. It seems I'm always about a half step behind. I've shot pictures of coyotes with the heads blurred and the tails sharp. But never hesitate to fire away when the subject is within range. You're going to waste some film, but that's the only way you'll ever get a picture. On a 36-exposure roll of film, if you get a half-dozen photos worth showing, consider yourself extremely fortunate. The count probably will be less. I've shot entire rolls without getting anything.

But even so, it's a lot of fun. When you attempt to maneuver a wild animal or bird into camera range, you'll begin to realize things you never were aware of before. Among other things, you'll find that every wild creature is an individual, with its own characteristics, its own peculiar ways. You never can predict how one will act or react.

I remember one individualistic bobcat. While it helped contribute to a most unusual photo, its unexpected behavior robbed me of many more, better pictures. I was hunting with my son, Hunter, on a cleared pipeline right-of-way in the south Texas brush. We were so well hidden it was unreal.

After several minutes of calling, a bobcat stepped into view and stopped about 40 feet away. I knew it probably wouldn't come closer, so I began snapping pictures. While doing this, I caught movement from the corner of my eye. Up the right-of-way came a coyote that was really picking 'em up and putting 'em down. I'd had this happen before, and normal operating procedure is for the bobcat to spook and run when it sees the coyote.

But this one stood its ground. It arched its back and bared its teeth as the coyote approached. I was so convinced the bobcat would run off that I didn't immediately start taking pictures of the two. When I did realize what was happening it was almost too late. The coyote stuck around only a second or two before leaving, then the bobcat took off.

I kept calling. In about five minutes, the coyote came back from

I prefer to steady my telephoto lens over an upturned knee.

the same direction in which he'd run away. How did I know it was the same coyote? Easy. If you observe wild animals, you realize that each one has a different look, as a rancher can distinguish one cow from another. I recognized this one right off.

I had a stuffed jackrabbit decoy in the clearing. When the coyote returned, it promptly sighted the rabbit and started circling it, so close to my position that I couldn't get the predator and fake prey into the same picture.

Of all the wild animals I've called and photographed, I suppose the fox is the most difficult. It's jittery, always moving about, and, because of its diminutive size, you have to have it real close to get much of a photo.

You'd think it would be harder to get a picture of a whitetail deer than it would a fox, but the opposite is true. The larger the animal, the easier your job, because the subject doesn't have to be nearly as close.

The coyote is about as difficult as the fox because of its suspicion. It's always alert to any danger. Even when they haven't been disturbed, coyotes are wild to the point of being paranoid. When one comes on a run, it usually leaves on a run, and it usually leaves in the same direction it came, knowing that direction to be safe.

When photographing wild animals, concealment is extra vital. The subject can't be aware of your presence. You learn from experience when you can and can't move. When the subject steps behind a bush, tree, or stump, you can make some fast adjustments to be ready when it steps back into the open.

You also have to be prepared. You can't lay the camera in your lap and, once the critter is in sight, hope to get it up and focused without being detected. I like to sit with a bush to my back, in complete camouflage, with upturned knees almost to my chin. I prefer a black camera body, and if there's any chrome on the camera or lens I cover it with camo tape. I rest the camera across my knees and I'm ready when something comes within range.

Mesh camo gloves might hinder you as you try to focus and snap the shutter. That's why it pays to work the controls at home with gloves on. Practice by trying to anticipate anything that might happen.

Among the easiest creatures to photograph are raccoons and owls. At night they'll come real close, but you'll have to use an artificial light source. That isn't a problem with a battery-powered compact flash that reaches way out, particularly if you're using a fast film and don't need that much light.

Yet, even with a flash, you'll need a telephoto lens—150mm being

If it comes within range, an owl is relatively easy to photograph.

the minimum, 200 or 300mm being even better. The 300mm lens should focus down to around 10 feet, however. This way you can completely fill the viewfinder with your subject. A 'coon or owl isn't that skittish; you usually have a brief time to put a bright light on it and quickly focus before activating the flash. With a 50mm lens you won't get much of anything, unless you have the animal or bird climb into your lap. In a compromising position like that, it's difficult to ask the subject to please say "Cheese."

Whitetail deer are reasonably easy to photograph, especially in the summer when a doe has young. I guess it's a protective mother instinct, but both whitetails and mule deer will come charging to a call that time of year. Often a doe comes close, almost too close.

She's really steamed up. You're probably better off to climb into a low fork of a tree before attempting to call. You never can predict what a crazy old doe will do.

Actually, all kinds of game can be photographed if you get in the woods with them. At certain times of the year, in certain weather conditions, rabbits will act almost tame. You easily can sneak close

I rattled antlers to bring this whitetail buck into camera range.

enough to a cottontail or jackrabbit to get its picture. But keep in mind that you'll never get a photo unless you're packing a camera that's handy enough to reach. Don't be hesitant to use it. Burn plenty of film. Practice is the only way to improve.

"What the heck," you might be thinking, "This stuff doesn't interest me—I'm not going to be taking pictures of any animals." But you're wrong. Think about it; even if you're not into live-animal photography, you probably take pictures of game you've killed. A lot of people send me snapshots of big deer they've killed or maybe a bobcat or coyote that was called. With few exceptions, the photos are of poor quality. A typical one will have a person holding up a bobcat in front of his home while he grins into the camera.

The best photos are taken in a natural setting where the game was killed. If it's a big-game animal like a deer or elk, I like to get a picture of the animal before it is gutted. It just looks a whole lot better. The problem is, often you don't have a camera right there on the spot. You have to wait until you get home. There's nothing deader looking than a dead animal being displayed in front of a building.

The solution is to carry a camera. Nowadays, this is no big deal. There are 35mm cameras not much larger than a pack of cigarettes. Put one in your jacket pocket so it's there when needed. I use a Minox, but there are many compact cameras as good. Such a camera is far superior to one that uses 110 film. With the 35mm camera, you can make a supersharp blowup to hang on the wall. Sure is cheaper than having the deer head mounted.

A typical compact camera won't have interchangeable lenses, but this feature really isn't needed. The camera is automatic, and some models even have autofocusing. It's difficult *not* to get a sharp, properly exposed picture. The only other feature I want is a self-timer. This way, if I'm hunting alone, I can place the camera on a rock or stump, anywhere it's steady, start the self-timer, step back, and snap my own picture.

I have a few suggestions to improve your photos greatly. First, move in close to your subject, completely filling the camera's viewfinder. You desire a picture of the subject, not all the wasted space around it. As you look through the viewfinder, be aware not only

A compact camera goes into a pocket and you've got it when you need it.

of your subject but what's behind it. Make the background as uncluttered as possible. Normally, you can get the desired background
by moving a few feet to the right or left. If you don't watch it,
you'll have a tree growing out of a human's head. Since a photo is
two dimensional, the background will be almost as prominent as
your subject is in the foreground. With most lenses, certainly the

wide-angle lenses on compact cameras (35mm or 28mm), the depth of field is great and the background will be sharp, making it even more distracting if it's cluttered. Keep any backdrop as plain and simple as possible.

And, finally, if you're photographing somebody with a dead animal, maybe a deer, have him doing something other than staring into the lens. Have him glancing at his kill rather than the camera. That's a big improvement. Talk to him as you snap away, getting him to relax. Many people "freeze" in front of a camera and appear ill at ease. Use your imagination and you'll get photos worthy of showing to your friends—photos they'll actually enjoy looking at.

Chapter 23

Calling for Profit

I've been hunting and trapping for longer than I can remember, and you could say I've sold my share of pelts. While I was in school this was about my only source of spending money. The amount of money I had to spend was in direct relation to the number of animals I'd hunted or trapped. My dad didn't give me anything. I earned it.

Looking back, that upbringing brought a lot of benefits. I know it made me a better hunter and trapper. The season was short and I had to collect enough pelts to bring in the few dollars I'd have to spread over the entire year. Since prices weren't all that good, that meant I had to get numbers. This was serious business.

It also taught me the importance of good management practices, keeping expenses to a minimum. I had a single-shot .22 and I made every cartridge count. Shooting at a tin can or a paper target was out of the question. So in the long run my upbringing made me a better shot.

And, for certain, I know it made me respect and appreciate wildlife. I used it but I didn't waste it. I always wanted some left for the next year. My family practically lived on wild game—squirrels, rabbits, and venison. But we never shot anything we couldn't use.

Fur-bearing animals are a renewable resource. I think we have more today of certain species than we did when I was a kid. I know we have more coyotes and I'd be willing to bet we also have more

The raccoon is plentiful and is one animal you can call for profit.

'coons. We definitely do in my part of the country. Regulated hunting is no threat to their numbers. The real threat is habitat destruction. If you take too many animals, nature has a way of compensating with a strong crop of young; but if you destroy the habitat, it takes years for it to recover, if ever. I've had it up to here with the do-gooder who hollers about saving the animals, then climbs on his bulldozer and begins clearing land for another shopping center. If it weren't for concerned hunters and trappers, we wouldn't have much wildlife anymore.

While many people still maintain trap lines, mostly as a sideline to make a little extra spending money, many also have found that they can call varmints for profit. While the fur prices fluctuate, in most years you can make some pretty good money by varmint calling in your spare time. You can have fun and get paid for it. That's a hard combination to beat.

Yet, even if prices are much higher for one animal than another, you'll probably make more money by concentrating on numbers. In most places the odds of calling four foxes or four 'coons are better than calling one bobcat, one reason being that foxes and raccoons are more plentiful, another being you don't have to stay in one place as long—you can make more calls in the same amount of time.

Another way to look at this is to take what's available. J. D. Taylor and I hunt together at least twice each winter. We try to determine, by scouting, what will result in the most dollars in the time we have to hunt. If 'coons are most prevalent, we concentrate mostly on 'coons. Or maybe there'll be more foxes. But even while targeting in on one species, we might call a bonus coyote or bobcat.

I also believe that if you have a variety of animals, you need to call in sequence. By this, I mean there is a logical order. For example, suppose my scouting indicates a good population of coyotes and 'coons, and some tracks indicate a few bobcats in the area. Where you have both coyotes and foxes, the coyotes tend to take the upper hand and the fox population dwindles, but 'coons and bobcats, on the other hand, will mix with both of them, and also with each other. As always, however, available food, of whatever kind, will dictate the type of species and numbers.

Okay, then, if you have coyotes, 'coons, and bobcats, you should start by calling the more open country in the daytime for coyotes. If you begin by calling at night, you'll only wise up the coyotes with not much chance of killing any. Thus, by making the coyotes more suspicious, your chances of calling one or more later, in the daytime, are much reduced. For coyote calling, you also should use a different sound than the one you'll subsequently try for 'coons and bobcats. Start with a lower-tone call and work up in pitch. After you've worked the coyotes over, you can concentrate on night calling—if it's legal in the area—for 'coons and bobcats using a higher-pitched call.

But calling is only part of it. It's important that the pelts receive proper care if you want to get top prices. It used to be that everyone stretched and dried their pelts for later sale. Nowadays, however, with fur buyers being so widespread and available, the easy way is to skin the animal properly and put the pelt in the deepfreeze until you're ready to sell it.

A varmint should be cased; that is, don't slit the hide along the animal's belly. I begin on the ground or a table, first chopping off the two forefeet. I've never met anyone else who does this, but it's a trick that makes skinning much easier. When you are stripping the hide, it will slide right off the forelegs with paws removed. Otherwise, in the skinning process, you have to pause and cut around the upper part of the paws to free the hide.

I'll slit the hindlegs down the inside, then get the hindquarters almost skinned before hanging the carcass by the hindlegs. Once the tail is stripped the rest of the skinning job doesn't take much time. When I get part of the tail bone exposed a couple of inches from the body, I take two sticks and put one on either side of the exposed part—one on the top, another on the bottom. Then, clamping the sticks together at both ends, I press them firmly against the tail bone. As I pull down steadily, the double-stick vise pushes or peels the tail off the bone. The procedure is very simple.

After that, I merely bring the skin down, over the front quarters and then the head. I put the pelt in some type of sealed container like a plastic bag or jar to keep the smell from contaminating everything else in the deepfreeze. But don't put the pelt into the container until you're ready to freeze it. Hang it up to cool. The sealed bag or jar can't breathe, so any body heat from the hide will get trapped inside. There's a good chance the pelt will spoil and the hair will start slipping.

I've always believed you should sell your pelts as you go along. Some people hold them until the end of the season, gambling that prices will go up. I've found that most of the time the opposite is

To skin a varmint, after cutting off the forefeet, I skin the hindlegs on the ground before hanging the animal.

I put a stick on either side of the tail bone, press the sticks together, and pull and peel the tail out.

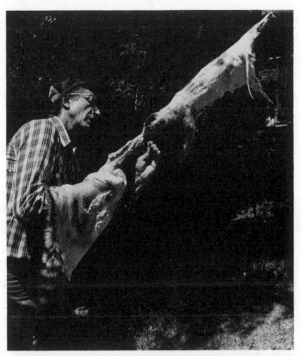

Then it's a simple procedure to skin all the way to the tip of the nose.

When I'm finished, I have a cased skin that's ready to go to the fur dealer or into the deepfreeze.

true, certainly during the years when varmints are plentiful and prices start out high. Near the end of the season, buyers have got about all they can handle. As a consequence, prices have fallen, sometimes more than half, or some buyers have quit buying altogether.

And for what it's worth, let me pass along this bit of advice. When I get invited to a place to hunt, I offer any pelts I get to the landowner or the hired help. Some take them, some don't. But the gesture is appreciated and I've found that I'm invited back. It's just good public relations, pure and simple. Respect every person's land and treat it better than you would your own.

If you think about it, winning over a landowner is the obvious first step in hunting. In states east of the Mississippi—and indeed even in parts of the Western states—most of the wildlife and quality hunting is on private lands. Get on a place and behave yourself and the word gets around. Don't feel that just because you're invited you can bring someone else. That's a quick way to wear out your welcome.

You've got to sell yourself. And unless you get through the gate onto lands where you can hunt, there's no reason to listen to me. Without a place to hunt, anything I've told you in this book isn't worth the paper it's printed on. Never forget that! Having a place to hunt is a privilege, one that is gradually being eroded because some hunters don't know how to behave themselves. And in the long run they ruin it for all of us.

Chapter 24

Calling in the Far North

One place where you can find plenty of uncrowded space in which to call is that part of the continent sprawling along the Arctic Circle, Alaska, and the upper reaches of Canada. It's also a prime location to call for profit. Because of the subfreezing winters, furs are luxuriant and bring premium prices.

Most of the Far North is isolated from much human traffic and perhaps that's a problem. Predators don't get much respect. People expect them to be naive and dumb.

Most everything I've heard from people who live in Alaska and northern Canada is they don't have any calling success. I suspect, however, some are having good success and they're keeping it to themselves.

I know I've called predators in the Far North. And from what I've observed, callers in this region are too casual. They think they can drive a few miles out of town and call something right away. It doesn't work that way. When animals live around civilization, they become more wary, smart to the human presence and how to stay hidden. It's just like blowing a call to a zoo animal; it won't pay any attention to you.

Even far from any road, the critters are wise to man's insidious intent. Find any area where a bush plane can put down in the wilderness and right there you'll have heavy trapping pressure. Trap-

The red fox is one animal that can be called for profit in the Far North.

ping is big business in the Far North, and it makes animals wise to humans.

Most residents of the far north don't realize this. I remember how Dick Hemmen acted the first time he and I went calling. We'd flown from Dick's hometown of Fairbanks southwest to the Wood River, about 50 miles upstream from its junction with the Tanana River. This is almost due east from Nenaha.

As I called, I noticed that Dick kept twisting and turning, looking back and forth. I could have spotted that much movement a mile away. Later, I told him that back home in Texas I was accustomed to hunting wild stuff. A person had to stay quiet and motionless. These Alaskan animals weren't a bunch of idiots. After that lecture, he got his act together and that's when we called both foxes and lynx.

Again, I think this is a matter of attitude. Just because a predator doesn't have a lot of contact with humans doesn't mean it's devoid

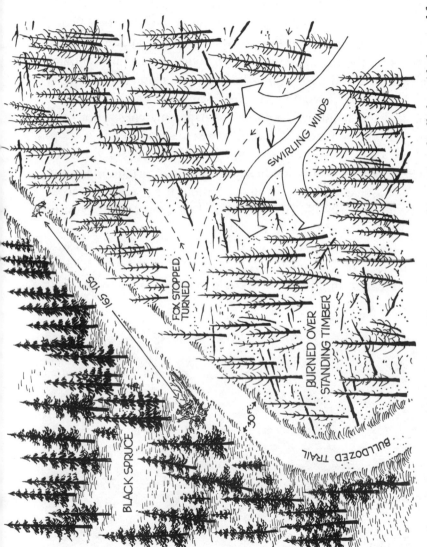

SWIRLING WINDS

165 YDS.

FOX STOPPED, TURNED

30 FT.

BURNED OVER STANDING TIMBER

BULLDOZED TRAIL

BLACK SPRUCE

This was the scene when I put the swirling wind to my advantage and called an Alaskan red fox.

of natural instincts. The person who's extra cautious and knows what he's doing is going to call something; the casual, haphazard caller who ignores the fundamentals is going to complain that a predator call won't work in Alaska or Canada. That's the difference.

Consider the unpredictable wind, as one example. When I tried to find a place to call along the Wood River, the biggest problem I had was overcoming the wind, which swirls around in the black spruce timber. If I'd tried calling before I got a precise reading of the wind direction, I would've been wasting my time.

I checked the wind with a folder of paper matches. In a burn area away from the timber, I walked about a 100-yard circle, stopping every 10 to 15 steps to strike a match, looking for the exact spot where the wind was holding steady out of a true direction. Once this was accomplished, I glanced about for a hiding place. A few steps away was a blown-down tree. I crawled up on it until I found sort of a natural seat in the roots.

Out in front of me was a green thicket that had escaped a forest fire in the area of a couple of years before. On either side were open areas where bulldozers had cut fire lanes, to keep the blaze

Notice how I keep my rifle ready so I can shoot quickly.

from spreading. Behind was virgin forest, but I really wasn't concerned about that since the wind was blowing my scent in that direction.

I started squeaking with my lips. In about five minutes I saw a fox running toward me over the rolling tundra, in and out of sight as it went through and over low and high places in the uneven terrain. The fox came fast and straight until it got within 40 yards. Just as I prepared to shoot, it winded me and took off in the opposite direction. The behavior reminded me of a smart coyote down in Texas. A predator is a predator no matter where you find it; the animal is just naturally suspicious.

The fox ran in a big circle and I kept calling. It passed through a thicket and came out in the fire lane to my left. The fox was 165 yards away—I stepped the distance off later.

When I first saw it break into the open, I picked my rifle up and plopped it over to the left. When the animal stopped, I already had my gun on it. But when I fired the animal sprinted away. The only way I knew it was hit was that it ran off in an unnatural manner, its tail straight up. It ran about 50 yards before going down. How

This is an Alaskan red fox that came to my call.

I still make mistakes. When we spotted a fox sunning in the snow, we stopped at the spot marked with an X and the animal saw us before we could call it. We should have slipped on around with the wind to our advantage, concealed ourselves, and then called.

it made it that far, I don't know. The .308 slug had completely destroyed the liver of the Alaskan red fox, a beautiful animal with rich, thick fur.

Now, considering what you've read previously, a .308 might seem a bit much for a fox. But there was a reason for the firepower. When scouting along the sandy Wood River I'd found an abundance of wildlife tracks—mink, lynx, fox, wolf, black bear, and grizzly bear. I've heard of hunters who were blowing on a predator call and suddenly had a grizzly appear. If that happened, I wanted to be prepared for any emergency. You don't take any chances with an unpredictable grizzly bear.

I like to think I outfoxed that fox by being a little bit smarter than it was. I'd slipped into the country and hidden without the animal knowing I was there. Trying to outguess the wind in fairly open country made the job more difficult, but I'd been careful. You have to rely on your best judgment to do everything right.

Later, I got a lynx for the same reason; I didn't take anything for granted. Dick and I sloshed about in the river bed until we located a likely spot to call. Small, winding branches broke away from the main river like splayed fingers and since I was wading in ordinary hunting boots, I was thankful that I had given them a liberal coating of waterproofing.

On a gravel bar in the river bed, I found a huge log that had been sandblasted white by flood waters. I knew this was as good a place as any, so Dick and I sat where we could lean against the log. I wore a white coat for camouflage.

The log was about 85 yards from the bordering timber—scattered alders backed by dense, tall spruce, their black trunks blending into what resembled a dark curtain. Conditions were near perfect; we had the wind to our favor and the sun at our backs. The angle of light would readily show up anything that emerged from the dark timber.

I commenced blowing on a WF-4 Burnham Bros. Deluxe Predator Call, made of walnut. This call has a deeper pitch than our plastic Long-Range Predator Call. I had the rifle rested across an upturned knee. If anything showed, all I had to do was flip off the safety and I was ready to fire.

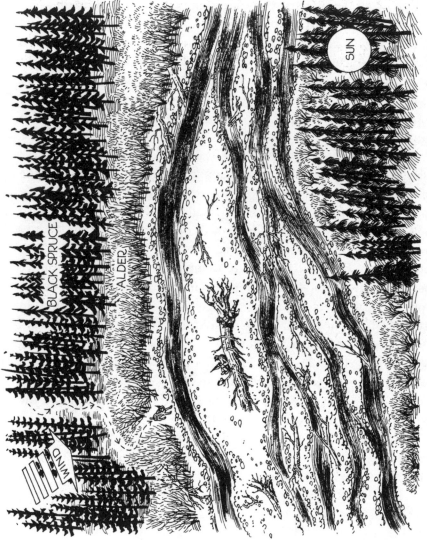

Dick Hemmen and I were hiding by an old log in the river bed, positioned where we could watch in all directions, when the lynx came out of the black spruce.

After calling for 10 minutes, I sighted movement. The cat came toward me in a swinging lope, out of the black spruce into the loose alders. When it ran into bright sunshine it stopped. I didn't try to bring it closer. This goes back to my philosophy to shoot when I think I have an animal dead. This lynx never knew what hit it.

The next day I called another lynx with a deer call. I also called another fox using lip squeaks. I don't think you'll call many foxes with a coarser call. They seem to prefer the high-pitched squeaking. Of course, these were the only animals Dick and I saw. We probably called more we didn't see. In fact, I'd bet on it. A caller normally brings in animals he never sees.

Although calling in a wilderness has certain advantages, it has drawbacks, as well. Dick and I were limited to hunting along the river. You don't strike out across the spongy tundra or snowshoe over a thick snow cover, whatever the conditions might be. Walking is too tough and you have to walk from one place to another. You can't just jump into a pickup and drive a mile to try again. Dick and I walked about 15 minutes between stops. We probably didn't have to go that far. Tall, thick timber muffles sound like a mountain. A call doesn't reach very far and you don't have to go that far between stops.

While calling in the Far North is different in some respects, the basics are the same. The terrain and conditions might be different, but the fundamentals aren't. Master the basics and do everything to the best of your ability and you can become a successful hunter, no matter where you live or visit.

Finally, as I said in the beginning, there are no shortcuts to success. You have to work at it. Me, I wouldn't have it any other way. I not only enjoy the challenge, I thrive on it.

Index